HOW TO TALK TO YOUR SON ABOUT FASCISM

How to Talk to Your Son about Fascism is a practical guide for parents, carers, and others with young men in their lives on how to talk with those young men about fascism and the right-wing, which specifically and particularly preys on them for recruitment.

Its central goal is to present research, history, and analysis about how and why the right-wing recruits young men to parents, educators, and anyone with a young person in their lives. The book covers the history of right-wing recruitment of young men, explaining why the right-wing focuses on recruiting men both on a theoretical basis and through the logic of movement-building, and then moves to practical analysis and suggestions for how to counter recruitment today. Recommendations come from excerpts and existing scholarship. Readers will come out of the book with a better understanding of what fascism is and how it works, how it preys on young men, how it recruits and appeals to them, and how to stop this from happening.

This book will be of interest to antifascist researchers and activists, as well as parents, carers, and the general reader concerned about the rise of the extreme right.

Craig A. Johnson is an independent journalist and an academic who hosts the podcast Fifteen Minutes of Fascism.

Routledge Studies in Fascism and the Far Right

Series editors: Nigel Copsey
Teesside University, UK
Graham Macklin
Center for Research on Extremism (C-REX), University of Oslo, Norway

This book series focuses upon national, transnational and global manifestations of fascist, far right and right-wing politics primarily within a historical context but also drawing on insights and approaches from other disciplinary perspectives. Its scope also includes anti-fascism, radical-right populism, extreme-right violence and terrorism, cultural manifestations of the far right, and points of convergence and exchange with the mainstream and traditional right.

Giving Credit to Dictatorship
Authoritarian Regimes and Financial Capitalism in Europe during the Twentieth Century
Edited by Valerio Torreggiani and José Luís Cardoso

Importing Fascism
The Italian Community's Fascist Experience in Interwar Scotland
Remigio Petrocelli

The Canadian Far-Right and Conspiracy Theories
Ahmed Al-Rawi, Carmen Celestini, Nicole K. Stewart, Joseph M. Nicolaï, and Nathan Worku

Building Dictatorships under Axis Rule
War, Military Occupation and Political Regimes
Edited by António Costa Pinto and Goffredo Adinolfi

How to Talk to Your Son about Fascism
Craig A. Johnson

For more information about this series, please visit: www.routledge.com/Routledge-Studies-in-Fascism-and-the-Far-Right/book-series/FFR

HOW TO TALK TO YOUR SON ABOUT FASCISM

Craig A. Johnson

R Routledge
Taylor & Francis Group

LONDON AND NEW YORK

Designed cover image: Getty images, credit: ilbusca

First published 2025
by Routledge
4 Park Square, Milton Park, Abingdon, Oxon OX14 4RN

and by Routledge
605 Third Avenue, New York, NY 10158

Routledge is an imprint of the Taylor & Francis Group, an informa business

© 2025 Craig A. Johnson

British Library Cataloguing-in-Publication Data
A catalogue record for this book is available from the British Library

ISBN: 978-1-032-47303-1 (hbk)
ISBN: 978-1-032-47253-9 (pbk)
ISBN: 978-1-003-38550-9 (ebk)

DOI: 10.4324/9781003385509

Typeset in Times New Roman
by Apex CoVantage, LLC

CONTENTS

ACKNOWLEDGMENTS

I would never have been able to write this book without the encouragement, help, and love from the people in my family and community. Specifically, I would like to thank Kris, Larry, and Kevin Johnson; Allxie Cleary; Avary Kent; Camille Villa; Ben Sigrist; Shayna Howlett; Laurel Chun; Brandon Ahlstrom; Joan Cleary; the dozens of experts I spoke to in preparation for writing this book; and countless others who expressed interest in the book and told me it was important work. I'm grateful to all of you, more than I can say.

ILLUSTRATIONS

Tables

Figures

INTRODUCTION

Caleb Cain was a young white man in 2014 who had recently dropped out of college. He was liberal, listless, and looking for community in rural West Virginia. Like many young people without a clear direction, he turned online to find a possible outlet for his need for social interaction.

By chance, and by the dictates of the YouTube algorithm, he found himself falling down what he came to call the "right-wing rabbit hole." He began to see more and more videos and other content that seemed to speak to him directly as he was— young, white, male, at the top of practically every social hierarchy but recognizing none of the benefits of it. This content told him that his problems were caused by women, by people of color, by Marxists, and by Jewish people.

Gradually he came to be shown more and more of this content, which seemed to reveal the secret behind how the world worked, in Cain's own words, "chasing uncomfortable truths."[1] This perception only accelerated with the victory of Donald Trump over Hillary Clinton in 2016, which Cain experienced as a moment of collective victory over the forces that had taken over his world and had denied him what he was due.

Cain never fell into the greatest extremes of right-wing ideology, but that didn't stop him from transforming his life. He alienated his old friends and shifted to a community of extreme conservatives. If he had continued on this trajectory, he could've very well ended up among those who stormed the US Capitol building on January 6 and be in jail today for sedition.

Fortunately for Cain, and for all the rest of us who want there to be less fascism in the world, he managed to de-radicalize himself and eventually became a speaker and activist against the radicalization of young men. But his success in saving himself from the right-wing cesspool isn't a reassuring story. Instead, it's a reminder that right-wing radicalization can happen to any young person, and in

DOI: 10.4324/9781003385509-1

the United States especially a young white man. In Caleb's own words, "literally anyone can be radicalized." Cain moderated his views in the late 2010s and even started his own YouTube channel whose original purpose was helping other young men de-radicalize themselves.[2] By the 2020s, he has tried to distance himself from the online world.

Hearing this story, you might find yourself wondering how this could have happened. How did an otherwise normal kid, raised in a good environment and with loving parents, turn to hate? In other words, how do young men become fascists?

News media and other sources will tell you that young men get radicalized on the internet. They'll say that the violence in the video games they play and the violent language used in gamer culture turn young men to the right-wing, or that the algorithms used by YouTube, TikTok, and other social media platforms emphasize and galvanize. There is something to this—gamer culture is a vector of far-right radicalization—but it can't be the only explanation. After all, young men joined fascist parties long before there was 4chan or Fortnite.[3]

If you turn to movies, books, and TV for answers, you'll probably be disappointed. Most stories that feature the right-wing shy away from telling you how and why people join it because it's depressing and frightening. Instead, when they do show it, it's like the person has contracted some inexplicable disease, like the messenger boy from "The Sound of Music," who goes from eliciting eye-rolls to holding a gun at the Von Trapps. This perpetuates the myth that the right-wing is something special and outside of our regular world, a comforting but incorrect thought.

Other sources will tell you that some young men join the right-wing by pathologizing both the young men and the right-wing itself. They'll point to psychologists or sociologists who look at young men who have committed acts of mass violence and explain them by means of their mental health.

These explanations of right-wing violence are especially prevalent immediately after a mass shooting or other act of violence. There's something to this narrative too—young men dealing with mental health crises or who feel lost in their communities are common targets for right-wing radicalization—but it can't explain how right-wing politics becomes so popular that it becomes normal. Saying that everyone in Italy, Romania, Spain, and Germany during the 1930s was mentally ill might be a reassuring way to avoid confronting how normal monstrous political thinking can become, but it won't help us confront the right-wing.

Instead, pathologizing right-wing youth is more likely to drive them further to the right-wing.

People will tell you that the media is to blame for this young man becoming a fascist. They might point to the rise of talking heads like Tucker Carlson, who has been spouting such terrible right-wing garbage that he's threatening to put openly fascist YouTubers out of business. They might say it's the constant coverage of fascist news or the fact that the news continues to give airtime to Donald Trump and his beliefs even after he openly tried to overthrow the government of the United

States. They might blame the "both-sides" coverage that most media outlets fall back on to avoid singling out the right-wing.

Other people will tell you that the real problem with young people and the right-wing comes from the internet—that its online forums, like Discord or video game chat rooms, are where young people learn to be fascists. They might point to websites like 4chan, which have long been safe places for right-wing thinking. Others will tell you that young men learn to be part of the right-wing from violent video games or games that have right-wing content.

I agree with a lot of these commentators. Online forums that allow fascism and video game communities that permit right-wing rhetoric do contribute to the growth of the right-wing and to young men's acceptance of fascism. But they aren't enough to explain why the right-wing is on the rise not just in the United States, or even the Western world, but almost everywhere in the world.

Our only way to confront this problem and stop the right-wing radicalization of young men is to look at it directly and honestly, and that means accepting some uncomfortable facts. One is that restricting a young person's access to media or the internet won't stop right-wing radicalization. Another is that many young men join right-wing groups independent of their mental well-being or their status in their community. Finally, and possibly scariest of all, is the fact that young men joining the right-wing is normal. It's normal now, it's been normal in the past, and it'll probably remain normal in the future. That means we have our work cut out for us if we want to stop the right-wing from growing. Young men are some of the biggest targets of right-wing recruiting today, and their recruits are getting younger and younger.[4] I wrote this book to help parents, educators, and anyone with a young man in their life keep them from falling too deep down the rabbit hole.

Consider this book an answer to these two questions—why do young men join the right-wing? And how can we stop them from doing it? Neither of these is a new question. People have been asking them for as long as there's been a right-wing. But this book will address these questions practically, with advice and strategies that you can use in your everyday life.

When I was a graduate student and would tell people I studied fascism, they'd often end the conversation by asking me what they can do to stop it. And there are a lot of things you can do! Vote against them when they run for office, be open with friends and family about your opposition to fascism, and work with big organizations that are opposing its rise. All of these have proven track records of stopping fascism from taking over countries or from heavily influencing them.

But there are other things we can do in our everyday lives that help stop the rise of fascism—and one of the most important of these is to stop the growth of their power base. As you'll learn by reading this book, that power base is overwhelmingly full of young men who belong to whatever ethnic, racial, or religious group constitutes the majority of their country. In India, this is Hindus; in Spain, it's

Catholics; and in the United States, it is white people. Fascists are also overwhelmingly male everywhere they appear. This has been true in the past, and it's true today, with groups like the Proud Boys, Patriot Front, and the Groypers consisting almost exclusively of men.

Many commentators have noted this before, and there have been a lot of good discussions about the work that white people, or men, need to do in their own communities and spaces to help slow or stop the rise of fascism. But there's been less attention to the fact that many fascists are *young*. This isn't to say that there aren't older fascists—like with any political movement, there's always an older generation that holds the wisdom from the past and educates the youth about it. But when it comes to new fascists, the majority of them are young.

That means that the youth of young men is a critical time to intervene and stop them from developing fascist politics or joining fascist organizations, so that instead of being influenced by fascist elders, they're influenced by antifascist ones. Recent studies have shown an uptick in concern over youth radicalization throughout the Western world.[5]

You can't just tell a 10-year-old it's his job to stop fascism. Despite his entry into the political world via an interest in fascism or the right-wing, he's still a child. He can't do that work on his own, without guidance. That work needs to start with his parents, educators, and caretakers. That's why I'm writing this book, and that's who it's for—it's for people who can notice that a young man is on the path to the radical right-wing and can talk him down from it, and for people who can help young men who aren't interested in the right-wing navigate a world where many of their peers will be expressing right-wing views. It's for anyone who has a young man—from about 10 to 25—in their lives. Parenting and childhood development books will tell you that these are critical years for brain and personality development in children and young people. It's for that very reason that they're critical years in their political development too, a vitally important time to steer a young man away from one of the most dangerous belief systems he could possibly follow. These are the years when young people's lives are the most malleable.

The right-wing is growing today in the United States and the rest of the world because many people feel that we are in a period of political upheaval. Things that people used to take for granted—jobs, housing, social structures—are in flux and no longer guaranteed. Most young people have grown up in a world where they can expect to live through climate catastrophes and generally worse economic conditions for themselves and their children than the ones their parents enjoyed. These looming disasters, combined with a lack of major social or political responses, leave many young people feeling hopeless.

Despite the fact that the world is, on average, safer and less violent now than it has ever been, and our lives are also, on average, wealthier and more stable than they've ever been, things do not seem that way to millions of people. This is important, because when it comes to politics, what matters isn't the facts; it's the *truth*. What matters is what people believe. Some people can be swayed by facts, but others simply can't. So because people perceive there to be a crisis, we're living through one.

If you don't believe we're in an economic or social crisis in the United States and the rest of the world, you might at least agree we're in a political one, and that the worst part of this crisis is the resurgence of extreme right-wing parties and movements. We see this in India, where the ruling party, the BJP, is part of an umbrella network called the RSS, arguably the biggest and most successful fascist organization after WWII. We see this in Hungary, where the ruling Fidesz party has become increasingly right-wing throughout the leadership of Viktor Orban, who has been positioning himself as the leader of a new international right-wing coalition. We see this in Italy, where a party descended from the Italian Fascist Party is now in government and pushing to reverse progressive trends in women's rights, LGBTQ rights, and the rights of immigrants.[6] In France, the National Front (now called the National Rally) has gotten closer to government than it's ever been before. In Germany, the Alternative for Germany Party (AfD) has weathered scandals and controversy over its connections to Nazism to outperform many centrist and center-left parties.[7] In Brazil, the government of Jair Bolsonaro ended with thousands of his supporters taking to the streets and attempting a coup on his behalf, while the Lula administration tries to root out examples of right-wing ideology in the military.

And then there's the United States, which over the last five years has seen its largest growth in fascist and far-right movements since the 1930s. The election of Donald Trump in 2016 was both the result and the cause of an upswell of right-wing ideology throughout the country. His success in the GOP primary was evidence of serious support for anti-immigrant, anti-queer, and anti-left politics more vitriolic than the previous GOP consensus reached under George W. Bush. And after his nomination, he used his platform to center ideas that would have previously been unspeakable by a leading figure in US politics—though the policies themselves that he implemented weren't entirely outside the norm, his rhetoric very much was.

Trump rode a groundswell of rising right-wing sentiment that was partly a result of ongoing social and economic crises and partly an openly racist response to the first Black President of the United States, Barack Obama. Trump's appearance on the national and international stage massively increased the right-wing's power. He gave legitimacy to right-wing views in the United States and inspired his followers to march en masse, hold rallies, and form smaller parties and organizations that hoped to take advantage of his reputation. The Unite the Right Rally of 2017 was a direct result of this increase in visibility and acceptability for the extreme right and fascism in particular. While that movement has so far proven unstable and has since fallen apart, the people it inspired, such as Nick Fuentes, are still very much the leading lights of the right-wing in the United States. Now that Trump has been reelected, this expression of the extreme right-wing is once again part of the governing coalition of the United States.

But the biggest problem for those of us who want to stop the growth of the right-wing is that when the fascists speak to men, they can say, with complete honesty, that men today have less power and influence than they used to. They can point to what everyone else, including mainstream conservatives, calls progress in racial, sexual, and gender inclusion and instead call it the erosion of men's social power. They can tell their supporters that things are harder for men today than they were in the 1970s or 1950s, and they're right. Relative to the rest of society, men earn less money, hold fewer political offices, own less property, and have fewer legal protections than they did in previous generations. For those who perceive politics as a zero-sum game where we are all fighting with each other for limited resources, that's reason enough to shift your political stance.

So, fascism is on the rise because the conditions are ripe for it. There's a genera-tion of young men who, honestly and accurately, can look into their future and see less power for them than their grandfathers had. They see fewer economic certain-ties, less social and political influence, and the rise of other demographics, which they might see as taking their power. Beyond that, they accurately see that many people born of the middle classes in the United States have worse economic pros-pects than their parents—they're likely to make less money and have less power, something called "downward mobility." We shouldn't be surprised that people looking at such a future might fight for something different. And, vitally, we can't be surprised if the thing they decide to fight for is selfish and destructive. Again, fascism is normal. It's what we can expect to rise from a political, economic, and social situation like the one we find ourselves in today.

So, what can we do about the rise of fascism? Just because it's predictable doesn't mean it's inevitable. There are things we can do—things *you* can do—to stop this from happening to the young people, and especially the young men, in your life. That's what this book is about.

Chapter 1 will explain what fascism is and how it fits into the wider network of the right-wing. It'll talk about historical fascism—the stuff you learned about in high school, like the Nazi Party—and also more recent right-wing groups like the modern KKK and the alt-right. The point of this chapter is to help you identify different parts of the right-wing and how they relate to each other, which is more important than memorizing one definition of "fascism" or "right-wing."

Chapter 2 builds on this introduction to fascism and the right-wing by explain-ing why fascists go after young men for recruitment. Again, there'll be some his-tory here, talking about groups like the Hitler Youth and other right-wing boys' clubs. But the focus will be on what it is about the right-wing that makes them recruit young men, and what it is about young men in our societies that makes the right-wing so appealing to so many of them. This is important information to help you understand why your son, or any young man in your life, might find himself associated with or interested in the right-wing.

Chapter 3 gets more practical by showing you *how* fascists go after young men. This chapter explains how young men get radicalized on the right-wing through relatives, friends, and online. All of these are important ways that young men become fascists, and eliminating one—say by blocking certain websites or by locking down a few apps—isn't enough to stop right-wing radicalization. Understanding how the right uses all the media, social, and political tools it has to radicalize young men is very important to stopping it. This chapter will cover important warning signs, symbols, and language that will help you identify when someone is getting recruited by the right-wing.

Chapter 4 is the heart of this book. It starts by telling you how to talk to your son, or any young man in your life, about fascism. It'll start with conversation and topic guides for people who want to talk to young men about fascism and the right-wing *before* they see warning signs. This is important because you have the best shot at preventing a young man from becoming a fascist if you get to him before they do.

Chapter 4 also tells you what to do if you are already worried that a young man is getting interested in the right-wing, or even if you know for sure that he is. This chapter includes conversation guides for how to talk to young men about the media they're consuming and ways to avoid being overbearing when talking to them about the right-wing. Remember that these conversations are some of the first adult ones you might have with a young man—you'll have to walk a balance between caretaking and respecting his independent opinions. Talking down to him about his beliefs, disparaging them, or distancing yourself will not help. Instead, this is a guide for how to treat your son as the equal he's becoming, learning to accept that his experiences are different from yours, and approaching his beliefs, even if they're dangerous or you disagree with them, with enough respect to keep him from dismissing you automatically.

This chapter will help you start conversations with your son before things get to that point, before he starts to exhibit an interest in fascism or the right-wing. Starting these conversations early, before he expresses any of those beliefs, is a vital part of preventing his radicalization—it'll help you establish your position relative to fascism, present yourself as a knowledgeable person he can trust talking to these things about, and will give you really important information about where your son is politically and socially. These are conversations you can have around the same time that you might start talking to your son about sex and reproductive health or about sexism and racism.

Chapter 5 addresses how to talk to young women and nonbinary people about fascism. In their case, it's more likely that these conversations will be about warning and solidarity rather than steering them clear of the extreme right, but it will also touch on how they can be radicalized toward fascism.

Chapter 6 concludes the book by showing how you and the young person in your life can be allies in fighting the rise of fascism in your community. It has helpful guides for what to do if you see fascist symbols or graffiti, or if you know that a fascist or otherwise extreme right-wing rally is being held near you. I've included testimony from people who safely and responsibly protest these events and guides for how to navigate them with children.

Beyond those direct forms of fighting fascism, this chapter also includes con-versation guides and best practices for you to help your son as he encounters peers who are expressing extreme right-wing sentiments. Showing your son that you trust him as a collaborator in this will help make sure that he sees fascism as a problem to be addressed, and it'll also let you know your family is doing its part to stop the increase in the number of fascist youths. Maybe most importantly, it'll help you and your son strategize about how he can respond to fascism and the extreme right-wing when you're not around—at school, with friends, and online.

Before I finish the introduction, I want to give some disclaimers. The first is about gender. In my everyday life, I avoid using gendered language when talking about strangers, so it's a little uncomfortable for me to only talk about young men and sons rather than young people or children. But I'm doing that, and writing the book this way, for a specific reason: young men are massively disproportionately targeted by the right-wing for recruitment, and not just in the present, but in the past too. Right-wing politics benefits men, and specifically cisgender men (as in, men who are not trans). Many people who study the right-wing, myself included, argue that the right-wing is sexist by nature in the same way that it's racist, nationalist, or violent.

Later chapters will cover the politics and history behind this in more detail, but fundamentally the reason I wrote this book with young men in mind rather than young people is that young men are more at risk for joining the right-wing. If you're the parent, caretaker, educator, or friend of a young person who isn't male, this book will still be useful to you, though. While I'll be focusing on right-wing recruitment of young men and how to stop it, this book will also help you identify when and how young men's behavior toward their peers of any gender represents more than our society's already terrible baseline of sexism and gender discrimina-tion and is verging on the extreme right-wing. It might help you understand what your daughter or child's peers, relatives, and friends are going through, or help you understand the dangers in their social world as a whole.

My last disclaimer is about politics. This book doesn't assume you identify with antifa or as a progressive, but it does assume that you think the far right is a politi-cal problem rather than something that our society should accept as normal. My goal isn't to convert you to one perspective or another—all I want is to give you the tools you need to keep young men away from fascism. Personally, I'm a leftist, but in the fight against fascism, groups from across the ideological spectrum have always come together and united to stop it. We've done it before, and we can do it again. I wrote this book as an invitation to anybody who is worried about fascism to join that fight so that we can win together.

I'm going to close out this introduction with this short guide to the whole book. If you've only got a few minutes, find yourself in a crisis situation, or want some reminders about the information I've laid out here, please dog-ear this page and come back to it.

First Steps

- Make sure that you and those around you are safe. You can't de-escalate anything with your son before you're sure that there isn't a danger to you or others in your home or community. Be especially careful if there's someone in your family who might be particularly vulnerable.
- Educate yourself about what right-wing radicalization looks like. Read this book, use other resources, and talk to your friends and family.

Things to Watch Out for in Your Son

- Big changes in friend groups, having only male friends
- Changes in the social media he's seeing—check for memes and content that touch on racist, sexist, or violent themes, even if they're supposedly doing so as a joke
- Not only telling inappropriate jokes (all young people push these boundaries), but *predominantly* telling inappropriate jokes—especially those that disparage women, people of color, and queer people
- Starting to use slurs he's never used before and not responding when you teach him that those words are unacceptable or do harm to others

Conversation Starters

- "Those aren't the kind of jokes I was telling when I was your age—where'd you hear them? What do you think is funny about them?"
- "Do you know the history behind the joke you just told or the meme you just showed me?"
- "Have you heard about this meme? Let me tell you about why some people think it's funny, and why I don't think it's funny."
- When they're learning about the Nazis/Mussolini/etc. in school: "Have you ever seen things on the internet/TikTok/etc. about that? How did you feel about it?"
- "What is it that you like about the content you're seeing? How does it make you feel?"
- Check in with your son about how he's feeling generally. Who are his friends, and what do they do together? What social needs does he have that maybe aren't being addressed?

Next Steps

- Keep asking questions about your son's social and media life. Make sure he knows that you love him and are there for him, but call him in on behaviors and talk that are connected with fascism and the extreme right-wing.

- Educate your son (and yourself!) about the dangers of fascism and the extreme right-wing in your town, your region, your country, and the world.
- Make a family plan for how you're going to fight fascism. Talk about voting, donations, signs in your yard, how to talk to friends and family, and participating in protests.

Notes

1 Gough, Sarah, "Caleb Cain: Former Far-Right Extremist Says 'No One Has a Strategy' for Ongoing Threat," *Sky News*, February 25, 2021.
2 Roose, Kevin, "The Making of a YouTube Radical," *New York Times*, June 8, 2019.
3 Schlegel, Linda, and Kowert, Rachel, eds., *Gaming and Extremism: The Radicalization of Digital Playgrounds*. New York: Routledge, 2024.
4 Davies, Jordan, and Davies, Emilia, "Terrorism: Police Concern Over Teen Far-Right Extremism," *BBC*, January 25, 2023.
5 Özerdem, Alpaslan, and Podder, Sukanya, "Disarming Youth Combatants: Mitigating Youth Radicalization and Violent Extremism," *Journal of Strategic Security* 4, no. 4 (2012): 63–80; Cherney, A., Belton, E., Norham, S. A. B., and Milts, J., "Understanding Youth Radicalisation: An Analysis of Australian Data," *Behavioral Sciences of Terrorism and Political Aggression* 14, no. 2 (2020): 97–119; Campelo, N., Oppetit, A., Neau, F., Cohen, D., and Bronsard, G., "Who Are the European Youths Willing to Engage in Radicalisation? A Multidisciplinary Review of Their Psychological and Social Profiles," *European Psychiatry* 52 (2018): 1–14.
6 Winfield, Nicole, "How a Party of Neo-Fascist Roots Won Big in Italy," *AP News*, September 26, 2022.
7 AP, "German Far-Right Party Reelects Its Leaders After Election Gains While Opponents Protest," *AP News*, June 29, 2024.

1

WHAT IS FASCISM?

If you want to stop fascism, you have to know what it is. This chapter connects fascism of the WWII era all the way to the present, from the Nazis to the Proud Boys. Understanding how to identify these groups and what they stand for are the first step in keeping their influence out of young men's lives. *That being said, if you are in an emergency situation, turn straight to Chapter Four!*

But defining fascism is a real problem—there are a lot of disagreements about what it is. The problem is that most of the time when people use the word "fascism," they just mean a political movement or government that they don't like or think is dangerous. This means that organizations as different as the KKK, the NYPD, Pinochet's dictatorship in Chile, and the Communist Party of China all get called fascists by people who don't like them.

But fascism isn't just an insult—it's a specific political alignment, and arming yourself with a clear definition will help you talk with a young man about why it's dangerous. Here it is:

Fascism: A nationalist, anti-liberal, sexist, and violent right-wing political movement that aims to remake the world.

Debates over this definition are important and worthwhile, but I'm going to stick with this one for the rest of this book.[1]

Fascism is a mass political movement on the right-wing. This means that it tends to be authoritarian and to have a single leader with a big personality, but also that it needs a large, organized group of people to be foot soldiers and local leaders. It also means that when fascists look around for political allies, they generally work with other people on the right-wing, like conservatives and libertarians, rather than people on the left, like liberals and socialists. Fascists don't care about liberating

DOI: 10.4324/9781003385509-2

the oppressed. They're interested in preserving the power of the people they think should naturally be in charge. In times of crisis, the mainstream right-wing looks to fascists as extra enforcement and as a potential threat to keep the left and center in line—this is how the Nazis ended up in charge of Germany. Other times, conservatives end up using and discarding the fascists once they've served their purpose.

Fascism is nationalist. That means that they think about politics in terms of nations rather than classes or interest groups. Fascists believe that their nation, whether they define it by religion, ethnicity, or race, is the best in the world. For most fascist regimes and movements in the United States and Europe, this means some form of white supremacy, but for fascists elsewhere, it may mean something entirely different. Most Indian fascists base their supremacist arguments on specific Hindu religious affiliation rather than race, and many Brazilian fascists in the 1930s focused on a combination of Catholicism and "Latin" culture.[2] Fascists also insist that while their nation is the strongest and best, it's also *currently* weak and downtrodden because of some outside force that's gotten inside them and corrupted them. For the Nazis, this was Jewish people. For the Italian Fascists, this was the other victorious countries in WWI, such as France and the United States. For the KKK, this was Black people and white Northerners. For the current fascists in the United States, this is a combination of LGBTQ people, non-white immigrants, Jewish people, and their "woke" allies. Fascists think that these other people don't belong in their communities and are less worthy of rights and privileges—or maybe that they aren't really people at all and should be exterminated.

Fascism is critical of the government. Fascists think that the government has been taken over by outside forces that have made it an illegitimate obstacle that can no longer be a force for good in the world. For the Nazis, this meant criticizing the republic that replaced the German Empire after their defeat in WWI, saying that the Jews had taken over the country and made them lose the war. For the Italians, this meant arguing that the Italian Parliament was indecisive and needed stronger leadership to bring the country back to its former glory. If you've ever heard someone talk about how the "Deep State" is keeping Trump or some other right-wing leader from doing what they want, they're demonstrating just this kind of thinking. In the United States, this can also mean claiming that Donald Trump actually won the 2020 election and that the Biden administration was an illegal fraud.

Fascism is revolutionary. Fascists believe that the current system of government and how our society works in general must be completely changed. They think that the government needs to be overthrown and replaced with one that is capable of dealing with the challenges they think are facing society. But they don't just want somebody else to be in charge of the system the way it is. Fascists don't stop at getting their candidate elected president or prime minister—they want to completely rewrite laws and transform the government from the ground up. This is one of the few traits that fascists share with the radical left.

Fascism is sexist. Like most people on the right-wing, fascists believe that there are certain spheres of life—like government, business, and anything with power—that are a natural environment for men and not for women. They think that women should be relegated to the world of family and childcare, and that they shouldn't have or want social power. Fascists think that this is both biologically obvious, since women are the ones who have children, and also politically and socially vital, since they think that anything that changes our society away from their imagined version of the past is wrong and needs to be counteracted. In recent years, fascists have also become more insistent that sex and gender are the same, denying the experience and existence of trans people.

Fascism is violent. While many political movements have agreed that violence can be *useful*, fascists believe that violence is *good*. They think that violence makes men into better men, and they believe that these violent men produce better futures. This love of violence is sometimes confusing to people who are unfamiliar with fascism, because it looks like other political movements that have also used violence to achieve their goals—like the IRA or even antifascists. The difference is that while other organizations might use violence as a means to an end, fascists think that violence *is* the goal. They've said this since the beginning of fascism, when Benito Mussolini claimed that he and his fellow WWI veterans were a new kind of man, a new breed of people whose job it was to cover the world with the violence they'd experienced in the trenches. Fascists participate in violence openly and happily. They physically fight each other for fun, engage in street violence, and start wars. Their belief in the power of violence is a major part of their revolutionary ideology, inspiring them to extreme lengths to get what they want.

Finally, fascism doesn't play by the rules. Fascists are willing to do whatever they think is necessary in order to take and maintain power. This sets them apart from mainstream conservatives and the rest of the right-wing, which play the game of normal politics in order to get what they want. Instead, fascists are willing to break rules in order to achieve their goals. They'll lie, openly violate the law, and stage coups in order to take or keep power. The fact that they play so dirty makes it hard to counteract them.

TABLE 1.1 will help clear up the differences between fascism and other political beliefs it often gets confused with. Like the definition I just gave you for fascism, this is meant to be a rough-and-ready, helpful guide, not a comprehensive explainer.

Fascism gets what it wants through a combination of normal electoral politics and organizing, as well as political violence. Sometimes fascists try to create political parties, but since the 1940s, they mostly stay smaller than that and form clubs, gangs, or factions inside bigger right-wing political parties. This can make identifying fascists among the rest of the right-wing extremely difficult.

One of the most complicated things about fascism is its relationship to the rest of the right-wing. I'm writing this book without assuming that you have any political affiliation or position other than not wanting your son to be a fascist, but I'm also not going to shy away from relating the connections between fascism and the rest of the right-wing. There's been a lot written about these connections.[3] The important

TABLE 1.1 Here's a helpful starting point for differentiating forms of right-wing politics, with some leftist politics thrown in for the sake of comparison.

Comparing movements	Fascism	Conservatism	Authoritarianism	Marxism	Liberalism
Mass movement	X	*		X	*
Right-wing	X	X	X		
Nationalist	X	X	X	*	*
Criticizes democracy	X		X	*	
Revolutionary	X			X	
Racism	X	*	*	*	*
Sexism	X	X	X	*	*
Believes violence is good	X		X		
Doesn't play by the rules	X			X	

Source: Author's creation.

* Indicates that this principle or belief isn't intrinsic to this group—such groups have the capacity to express this policy or politics, but it isn't a necessary part of the politics or policies associated with these umbrella terms.

thing for you to know is that conservatives use fascists as a hit squad to do the dirty work their supporters won't, or that they don't want to be caught being connected to.

By "dirty work," I mean violence—street fights, assassinations, and intimidation. Nazi paramilitaries helped German conservatives stop union and Communist organizing. The KKK was a tool for the Southern white establishment, doing dirty work that they didn't want to be officially associated with.

A more recent example is the connection between former President Donald Trump and the fascist groups that invaded the US Capitol on January 6, 2021. Trump, himself a complicated figure on the right-wing, was always willing to spout the ideology and perspective of the far-right without being *directly* associated with it. He mostly avoided meeting with their leaders before the coup and dealt with them through proxies.[4] This has proven to be vitally important to the legal cases he is facing now that he's being investigated for the January 6 attempted coup, as he can claim to have not been directly involved in their storming of the Capitol despite his having very directly urged them to do so.

But this relationship between fascists and conservatives goes both ways. While conservatives are using fascists to do their dirty work, fascists are using conservatives to gain momentum and legitimacy. Returning to the Donald Trump example, fascist supporters of his presidency could point to many of his comments as legitimizing their actions. They could reference their connections to claim that they were working with the administration. Fascists intentionally blur the differences between their movement and mainstream conservatives.

It is sometimes difficult to be completely sure whether someone is a fascist—it's usually not as obvious as them wearing a swastika armband or giving the Nazi salute. Most of the time, it's a matter of paying close attention to their words and arguments, making connections to historical examples, and taking advice and perspective from people who study them.

Now, I don't want you to limit yourself based on a definition! If you're worried about a young man in your life and think that he's being radicalized by the right-wing, don't sigh with relief if it turns out he's calling for the restoration of the Confederate States of America instead of being a neo-Nazi! Those are both dangerous right-wing movements that can draw young men into worlds of physical and rhetorical violence. This path, from saying slurs to joining paramilitary organizations, buying guns and weapons, and engaging in bloody violence, can lead them to prison or death. That's why the strategies and perspectives in this book apply to whatever right-wing ideology the young man you're concerned about is interested in or subscribing to.

For the purposes of this book, we can proceed based on the assumption that if it quacks like a duck, it's a duck. If you encounter a person or a politician who is racist, sexist, revolutionary, right-wing, and violent, just go ahead and call them a fascist.

History of Fascism

Fascism originated in Europe just over 100 years ago, right after the First World War (WWI). At first, these early fascists were men who had fought in the war and used that fact as the basis for their whole identity and politics. Benito Mussolini created the Fascist Party based on ideas he developed while serving in the trenches of WWI. He thought that the war had created a new, more violent, and more powerful kind of man who was the right kind of leader for the new century. The Nazi Party in Germany grew from groups of veterans who had been taking to the streets to express their violent urges and their right-wing politics, mostly targeting socialists, communists, and other leftists. Both the Italian Fascists and the German Nazis directed their violence at the political left, attacking socialists and communists with street violence, assassinations, and other forms of brutality.

Fascists grew their ranks through a combination of street-level violence and electioneering, fighting their opponents at the ballot box and with fists and weapons. This was a potent and common combination in the early 20th century and won them real successes around the world. Up to the outbreak of WWII, many people all over the world admired fascists for their successful movement building and their political work, turning around the economies and nations of the losers in WWI. Some of their fans sought to emulate them by founding their own, smaller parties.

Then, just like now, there were small fascist organizations literally everywhere, in many major cities and in most countries from Chile to Canada, from the United

Kingdom to the USSR. In the United States, there was the second KKK, tens of thousands of white men in the South and the Midwest who campaigned against immigrants, Catholics, Jewish people, and Black people. In the United Kingdom, there was Oswald Mosley's British Union of Fascists. In Brazil, there were the Integralists, who fought in the name of Catholic nationalism. All of these groups mimicked the European fascists with uniforms, big rallies, fiery speeches, and street violence.[5]

Fascism wasn't a strange political disease that afflicted Germany and Italy—it was a global movement that appealed to millions of people all over the world. Here is the story of one of them.

Horst Wessel was born in 1907 in northwestern Germany to a family dominated by Lutheran ministers. His father served as a Lutheran minister, and his mother stayed at home raising him and his younger siblings. The family moved to Berlin in the early 1910s, where his father continued his ministry. At the urging of his father, Wessel joined the youth wing of what was at the time Germany's largest right-wing political organization, the German National People's Party. However, once he was 18 and no longer under his parents' thumb, Wessel left the People's Party and began his descent into the extreme right.

He began going to rowdy bars to meet other dissatisfied youth. This was 1925, and the German economy was collapsing around these young men. They experienced inflation rates of up to 350% per month as their country's government and economy were hobbled by sanctions imposed on the defeated German Empire after WWI. These young men looked into the future and saw their lives worse than their parents' were, the perfect breeding ground for right-wing sentiments.

Like many of these other young Germans, Wessel spent the next few years joining and then leaving various paramilitary factions. He joined the Viking League, a militant right-wing organization run by a former German naval officer, as well as other groups that were openly anti-Semitic, openly opposed to democracy, and interested in what they called "national renewal" and "raising boys to be real German men."[6] Wessel earned a reputation as a tactician and leader, rallying his fellow young men to fight Communists and Socialists in the streets.

These smaller groups eventually lost out to the Nazi Party. Wessel joined the Nazis in early December 1926, motivated by the group's rising power and the fact that many of his former comrades from other paramilitary groups had already signed up. Wessel, being a young radical eager for street violence, joined the paramilitary wing of the Nazi Party, the Sturmabteilung, or SA.[7]

Wessel was not alone in his experience with the German far-right. Thousands of young German men joined these paramilitaries. Eventually, the Nazi Party would force all young men to participate in this radicalization via the Hitler Youth. The Hitler Youth and the other groups that came before it indoctrinated young men in white supremacy, male supremacy, anti-Semitism, anti-socialism, anti-communism, and trained them in physical and armed combat. Echoes of this form of youth organization can be seen today in fascist organizations such as the

BJP's own youth wing, the Indian People's Youth Front, or the Patriot Front of the United States.

Wessel excelled in the Nazi Party. He was an effective leader and a good mentee for the head of the Berlin SA, Joseph Goebbels, who would later become one of the leading figures of the Nazi government. Wessel was arrested for the first time in 1927, after returning to Berlin from a Nazi rally in Nuremberg. After this, Wessel increasingly abandoned his regular life and his studies to devote all his time to Nazi Party activities. He visited other cities with Nazi Party organizations to work with higher-ups and to teach other young men how to lead street-level conflict. As the leader of his SA district, Wessel developed a reputation for ruthless violence and political influence, effective both in a street brawl and at giving a speech to a crowd of young Nazis. He was also a capable propagandist, writing the song "Raise the Flag," which would eventually become the anthem of the Nazi Party.

Wessel perfectly blended the violence and terrorism of the Nazi Party with its ambitions to actually govern. He was identified by Nazi elders as a candidate for real leadership and spoke at Nazi events in Berlin weekly, while developing a reputation as the leader of the most violent of the Nazi gangs in the city. Wessel was going places in the party, and it must have seemed to him that abandoning his studies and his former life was going to pay off.

He was wrong, though—before he could reach the political heights he clearly dreamed of, he was shot by a Communist militant in 1930. Wessel died slowly, not of the gunshot but from blood poisoning during his hospital stay.

Now dead, Wessel was even more powerful propaganda. His murderers were identified as Communists long before they were arrested, and his death became a rallying cry for other Nazi youth. Goebbels particularly, the head of the Nazi propaganda machine and one of Wessel's closest mentors in the movement, immediately capitalized on Wessel's death and pushed the idea of his being a martyr for the Nazi cause, a young man who gave everything for his party and his country. The Nazis filmed his funeral and made it the center of a propaganda push—Goebbels himself, rather than any of Wessel's relatives, gave the eulogy.

Thereafter, Wessel became a symbol of Nazi power and sacrifice. The song he wrote to prepare his fellow youth for street violence became an anthem of the Nazi Party, and his grave in Berlin became a site of pilgrimage for Nazi youth leaders. After the war, his grave and those of his family were vandalized and destroyed by antifascists hoping to eliminate another place that neo-Nazi organizations could rally support.

Wessel, like many others who looked to the right-wing as a place where they might belong, never grew up. We can't know if he would have turned on his ideology or regretted his actions later in life. If the behavior of his mentor Joseph Goebbels is any indication, we can guess that if he'd lived on through to the end of WWII, he might have been afraid of prosecution and killed himself before he was caught by the Allies and put on trial for his crimes.

Wessel's short life has a lot to teach those of us who are worried about young men becoming fascists. In just a few short years, he fell so completely into the world of right-wing street violence that it became his entire identity. He dropped out of school, left his everyday life, and devoted all his energies to the movement. And after he died, his identity as a fascist eclipsed everything else important about his family and his life.

His trajectory tells us that parents worried about their sons have to act to prevent their radicalization before it goes too far and that they can't accept it or go along with it, thinking that their sons are just looking for community and are happy to find it anywhere. Instead, you need to see interest in fascism as an indication that your son lacks other healthy community engagement outlets. That's exactly what this book will help you do—to keep your son from falling so far down a right-wing rabbit hole that he becomes a danger to himself and others.

Why Do People Become Fascists?

Hitler didn't win power in Germany advocating for mass murder or for attacking the Soviet Union—he did it by blaming Jewish people and Communists for causing Germany's problems and proposing to construct a new national unity centered on his vision of white, Aryan identity. Similarly, Mussolini took power in Italy not by saying that he would work with other fascists to achieve international fascist dominance—he did it by pointing out real problems that large sectors of the Italian people were having with their economy and government, which other parties addressed inadequately or not at all.

Other fascist groups were broadly similar, combining racist propaganda about their preferred ethnic, religious, or political enemies with economic and political promises. Fascists and those who work with them don't think they're the bad guys. They don't think fascism is evil, and they don't experience it as the absence of civil society or as a negative force in the world. For them, fascism is a community and a force for good.

This is the extremely simple answer to the otherwise bewildering question of how people could possibly believe in or do the awful things the Nazis did. The answer is that these ideologies and movements didn't start off advocating for the wholesale murder of millions of people. They began by providing a place for disaffected people who felt that they weren't being well represented by anybody on the political spectrum. Fascism appealed to people because it claimed that it could improve their lives.

And they weren't lying! Fascist parties from the 1920s-40s did materially improve the lives of their followers after they took power, partly by following through on their plans to reorganize their countries' economies, partly by capitalizing on the improving economy of the world as a whole, and partly by stealing from people they looked down on.

Contrary to most media depictions of fascism, where people are forced to fall in line, fascism instead worked in almost the exact opposite way. People weren't forced to join fascist parties. In fact, membership was limited, especially after they'd taken power. Being a party member, and especially having joined early, was an important way to signal your importance in Germany and Italy. It meant getting jobs, government contracts, or important meetings with influential people. It meant prestige and privilege. People petitioned and applied, and even begged for membership, desperate to participate in the political system that seemed like it was heading for the future.

The simple truth is that many people *wanted* to be fascists. The parents of young men were proud to see them in uniform. They were prizes on the dating market, the face of the nation, and were launching their people into the future. Fascism was new, exciting, and active. It captured peoples' imaginations, even beyond politics. It inspired artists, authors, and filmmakers. It was, in a word, popular.

Partly because it's so violent and dangerous, and partly because it seems so evil, most accounts of fascism tell a story in which fascism just *happens* to societies when something has gone horribly wrong. Everyday people are forced to join up with the fascists, who are somehow both very powerful and also unpopular. Fascism is painted as the failure of civil society, the failure of government, or the failure of normal elites.

But fascism is none of these things—we can't dismiss it as a ploy to manipulate the masses, or an example of society's death. Instead, it's an example of the incredible *success* of major social organizations, namely fascist parties and social movements. Failing to think about fascist movements as something that might be appealing to their members, rather than something that's imposed on them from above, is one of the main problems with fighting fascism. If you can't understand why a person might be excited about or interested in fascism, you won't be able to steer him away from it.

Fascism and Civil Society

There's a theory about fascism that has become common sense, and it's probably the one that you've heard of or thought of yourself. An endless stream of books, articles, and podcasts written by political commentators and former political staffers will tell you that fascism comes from an absence of what social scientists call "civil society."

Civil society is an umbrella term that means all the little groups, voluntary associations, just-for-fun sports leagues, church meetings, and clubs that exist in a society. It's any group of people that get together because of a shared interest or goal outside of education, work, or the government—so your daily standup meeting at work doesn't count, but the weekly after-office drinks at the local bar do.

Most academics agree that having a robust and interlocking civil society makes a culture better and more resilient to emergencies. It means that people have deep connections to their communities that they can rely on in times of crisis, and that those connections are ones that they've chosen rather than ones that were put on them by work or school. The idea is that when a community has a strong civil society component, fewer people fall through the cracks because it's easier for them to be picked up by the people around them. A mom's support group might help out a single parent who can't afford childcare during an emergency, or a church group might pool resources together to keep someone financially afloat to prevent them from being evicted. Friends from a sports league might help you get references to get a job or write a letter of recommendation for your kid. And on an even more mundane level, civil society just makes a community feel more alive and wholesome, a little more like an actual community rather than just a collection of people.

Civil society is on the decline throughout most of the Western world. The simple fact is that fewer and fewer people are members of these kinds of organizations, and they've been shrinking for several decades. I'm sure you can think of examples of this in your personal life or in your own community—empty churches, abandoned former Elks or Knights of Columbus lodges, once vibrant clubs that are now full of older people who complain that younger folks no longer want to join.

You might have heard this story before—it's something that regularly gets writeups in publications like the *New York Times* or coverage on CNN. Sometimes the culprit is the internet, sometimes it's the decline in church attendance, and sometimes it's an ill-defined modern malaise, but the idea is that our society is crumbling before our eyes and that we're all much more alone than we were before. Scholars have written many books and done a lot of research suggesting that the loss of civil society has resulted in people feeling more depressed and lonelier than they used to.[8]

Often, this decline in civil society gets blamed for the rise of polarization and extremism. People are less associated with each other, which means that they're less interested in each other's lives, which leads them to be less caring and connected, which causes the rise of politics that are oppressive and uncaring, like fascism, sexism, and white supremacism. Common sense agrees with this. Anyone who isn't a fascist will likely look at those who have developed this ideology and wonder how or why they might have fallen so far or lost some human, caring part of themselves that would prevent them from developing this hateful politics.

Unfortunately, the reality is more complicated than that.

If we look back in history, we'll see that extremist movements and ideologies have existed for a long time and that they long predate the social change that's used to explain them. After all, groups like the KKK and the Nazi Party emerged when the United States and Europe were so full of civil society organizations that imagining their absence would have seemed like the end of civilization itself.

Professor Dylan Riley at UC Berkeley has thrown another wrench in this story. His work studies the growth of fascist parties in several European countries and shows that, contrary to popular belief, it was in the places that had *stronger* civil society organizations that fascism was most successful—in other words, the exact opposite of the common-sense belief that strong civil society prevents fascism and other extremism. Riley showed this by looking at the growth and appeal of several fascist parties in the 1930s and found that they were the strongest in regions of Europe where civil society groups were the thickest and most interconnected.

It's not just that fascism grows best where civil society is strongest. Fascism *itself* is a powerful form of civil society. What is a fascist organization if not a voluntary association of people coming together because of some common cause? The concept of civil society usually doesn't include openly political groups, but the fascist parties of the 1920s and '30s certainly performed a lot of the same functions as civil society organizations. They provided spaces where people could meet and socialize. They performed civic functions like helping people get jobs, giving people power and influence in their communities, and advocating for their members against the rest of society. Most importantly, they also gave people a real sense of belonging.

So when you think about fascism, don't think about it some kind of empty, evil space that can only be filled with monsters who have lost their hearts and souls. Fascism is a political movement built in exactly the same way as any other—by giving the people in it a sense of belonging and purpose, a meaningful community to join, and a clear set of goals for the future.

This is one of the greatest dangers that fascism poses, especially for isolated, disaffected, lonely young people. Aside from their violence and angry rhetoric, they offer young men something real: community.

Fascism After WWII

After WWII, fascism was defeated and out of favor throughout most of the Western world. In many countries in Europe, expressing sympathy for the fascist parties that had just a few decades ago been extremely popular, or even in control, was now completely illegal. People who had participated in those governments were put on trial for their crimes against humanity and their fellow citizens. Many of them served long prison sentences, and some of them were executed. The symbols and slogans of the parties were also suppressed—to this day it is illegal to fly the Nazi flag in Germany. Those who weren't sent to jail or killed for their involvement in these regimes and parties had their lives tainted by that past, and while some of them didn't face the serious consequences they deserved, they at least had to live with the utter defeat of this program they so earnestly believed in.

Even in countries like Spain and Portugal, which were controlled by the far right and remained neutral and undefeated throughout the war, the fascists were sidelined by the 1950s in favor of bureaucrats who could engage with the democratic nations. Just as before the war, there were small fascist groups operating all over Europe and the Americas, but these groups were small and not that important. This meant that fascism spent most of the mid-20th century being a marginal, small group on the outside of power, with a few notable exceptions.

Since WWII was the story of fascism's defeat, the story of its comeback starts about a decade later with the emergence of what most observers call "neo-Nazism" or "neo-fascism." This new fascism was different depending on whether the country had been ruled by the fascists or not. In countries that were run by the fascists, such as Germany, Austria, Italy, and Romania, these groups often became political parties founded and staffed by fascists who made it out of the postwar purges unscathed and were still able to participate in political life. One example of these parties include the Freedom Party in Austria, whose founder was a Nazi and SS officer. Some of these parties are incredibly successful today—as I write this, one such party, the Brothers of Italy, is currently the governing party in the Italian Parliament.

For most of these groups, their fascist lineage was an open secret. Many of their members were secondary or lesser functionaries from the fascist era, or were the children or relatives of those people. In Italy and Germany, they had to be careful to work around the laws that those countries had passed after the war that made open fascist organizing a serious crime.

Neo-Naziism wasn't popular in the United States or the United Kingdom in the 1940s and 50s. Millions of young men had served in their country's militaries fighting the Germans, and hundreds of thousands had died to defeat fascism. But by the 1960s and 1970s, there were new generations of young men who hadn't risked their lives or lost their friends in fighting Germany and Italy. Some of these young men—not a lot of them, but some of them—turned to the extreme right-wing as a means of setting themselves apart from their fellow youth.

These early neo-fascist movements often looked like direct imitations of the WWII-era fascist organizations. They'd dress up in their own versions of fascist uniforms, hold rallies in the style of the fascist militants from decades ago, and use the same slogans. Often they'd have to change their logos and some other symbols, as the ones that had been used by the fascists were illegal—for example, the swastika has been basically illegal to display in Germany since the 1950s. These groups remained small and relatively uninfluential, except for occasional involvement in street violence or a protest that went wrong.

By the 1970s, though, things had changed. Many young men were no longer interested in joining the old party organizations and turned instead to increasingly violent and disorganized groups of thugs. Many of these people became what we now call "skinheads."

Though now synonymous with fascism and racism, the word skinhead used to refer to something else. Skinheads were a youth subculture originating in the working class of England in the 1960s, where young men who worked in factories and other manual labor jobs felt left out of most counterculture trends. Rather than going to college, wearing long hair, and dropping out of society, they adopted a utilitarian look—jeans and working boots due to the physical nature of their jobs, shaved heads to avoid hair getting caught in machinery. They also directly worked with the increasing numbers of immigrants from the UK's Caribbean colonies, predominantly Black men and women who brought with them new food, music, and dances. Because of this, early skinhead culture was actually anti-racist by nature, focusing on cooperation between white and Black communities.

But by the 1970s and 1980s, skinheads were increasingly listening to punk and other forms of music that were predominantly produced by white artists. Eventually, the word skinhead came to mean someone who was a right-winger, someone who supported white nationalism, someone who was a fascist. This was partly due to the socioeconomic changes in the United Kingdom under Margaret Thatcher, as she pitted the working class against itself and fostered racism. But it was also due to the successful organizing by neo-Nazis, who saw in the skinheads a group of angry young men who saw themselves without a future to look forward to but who were already organized in a subculture together—a ripe target for political organizing! Today, if you say "skinhead," the only thing that comes to mind is an angry, bald white man in big black boots giving a Nazi salute.

I spoke with Tony McAller, one of the most influential skinhead fascists in the 1980s, who has since left the movement and become an influential former fascist who works to keep kids out of the extreme right-wing. Our conversation drove home the truth behind how young men get into fascism. McAller was calm and confident when talking about his past, something I didn't expect from a former neo-Nazi militant and activist, especially not one who was so much in the limelight.

Living in Canada with English parents, he found himself turning to his English heritage as a way to connect with his emotionally and often physically distant father. "[T]he intense English working-class skinhead culture started to feel more real" as he grew older.[9] This longing for identity and belonging developed into an identity crisis. With the punk scene in full swing, McAller turned to music and concerts as a place to find himself and his friends. The aggressive lyrics and rhythms appealed to him as a young man who felt restless and listless, and he spent many nights losing himself and his self-doubt dancing violently in clubs and bars. At the time, the punk scene was also a place where right-wing skinheads organized. With their shaved heads and violent, racist politics, they found the disaffected young men of the scene to be a perfect place to recruit.

Well-spoken and well-educated, McAller wasn't your stereotypical neo-Nazi. "My voice was my weapon of choice," he says now of his time as a leader of fascist movements. This isn't to say that he didn't participate in violence—you couldn't be a legitimate leader of your fellow fascists if you steered clear of violence altogether—but his role wasn't that of enforcer. Instead, McAller's aim was to get people into arguments about the Holocaust, or Hitler, or contemporary politics and to hit them with things they didn't know or questions they hadn't considered. His goal was to surprise people who expected a dumb, angry skinhead with his debate skills and knowledge.

There were many times in his life when members of his family and social circle tried to keep McAller out of fascism. "That's why my father threw me out of the house," he says, to punish him for joining these groups. But that just drove him further into the world of white supremacy, as he no longer felt that he had a family or community other than the one he had built around fascist politics. He did stay in touch with his mother, who continued to speak with him and tell him how much she disapproved of his social and political life. That connection to the outside world would prove to be incredibly important to him later.

McAller went on to become one of the most influential and well-connected fascists in North America. He attended conferences of extreme right-wing ideologues, rubbing shoulders with neo-Nazi political parties, white nationalist Christian groups, and the Ku Klux Klan, generally as a representative of the new generation of right-wing politicized skinheads. He pioneered new ways of communicating with other white nationalists, starting the first fascist phone network in Canada using what was an innovative technology in the 1980s that allowed the user to choose phone messages from a menu on a programmed answering machine. Callers could say they wanted more information about "Zionist conspiracies" or about "race science" and get long pre-programmed messages about them.

This allowed him to spread neo-Nazi ideology to potential followers and interested people passively and much more personally than handing out literature or trying to engage them in a conversation about fascism. His ownership of this service landed him in a Canadian courtroom for the spread of racially hateful messaging—ultimately, he was allowed to continue the service but with a curtailed message that met censorship requirements.

That was McAller as an individual fascist innovator—as a collaborator, he attended the rallies and events of other fascist groups, tried to get more teenagers and young men involved in the movement, and was some of the "glue" that held together the fascist movement in Canada and the United States. He even suspects that one of the characters in "American History X," the 1998 movie about neo-Nazis organizing in Orange County, is based on him—both he and the character in question were pest exterminators by trade, and both made jokes about their job and the Holocaust, something he was known for when he was a fascist.

McAller made it out of neo-Nazism alive but had lost a marriage and jeopardized his relationship with his family during his time on the far right. And that's saying nothing about the suffering, pain, and violence he caused to others, or the people he converted to his cause.

Fascists in the United States Today

Since the 1990s, we've seen more and more fascist movements and people gaining influence in the United States and elsewhere. There are many reasons for this—one is that the internet has made it easier for members of fringe groups to get in touch with each other, making organizing and sharing their opinions much simpler. In the 90s, we saw big fascist websites, like Stormfront, acting as beacons and rallying points for fascist sympathizers. These websites and the communities they produced made a power base for fascists that they could use to engage in real-world organizing. The growth of fascist movements and messaging on today's online platforms, like YouTube and TikTok, is part of this same trend.

But these technologies aren't the only reason, or even the main reason, that fascists are growing in power and prevalence today. As I'll say in greater depth in Chapter 2, fascism *uses* technology to grow, but it doesn't rely on any particular format or new innovation to increase its power. The central reason that fascists are growing in power today is that conditions are ripe for them to expand.

In both the early 20th century and today, fascists take advantage of real social and economic problems, twisting them to blame victims for the suffering of people who used to be more privileged. Historians call these people—who used to have more power in society but who are seeing that power fade—"downwardly mobile." This can happen to a group of people for two main reasons.

One is that the standard of living in their society is declining on average. This is what happened in Germany before the Nazis took power, for example: the economy tanked, and millions of people found themselves much worse off than they had been before WWI. This let the Nazis come in and blame the problems people were experiencing on democracy, communists, and Jewish people, rather than on the real causes of their problems, which were international business cycles and the greed and pride of their former Imperial German leaders for engaging in a war of aggression.

The other way that a group of people can be "downwardly mobile" is if their fortunes are falling relative to other groups, *even if* their standards of living are, on average, higher than they used to be. This can look like the "rising tide raises all ships," as standards of living improve for everyone in a society over time. More worrying, though, is if the privileged people are losing their old position relative to oppressed people who are gaining more power. In those situations, the privileged people can correctly say that the ways that society is changing mean that they will have less power than their parents and grandparents did, and even argue that their lives might be worse than if they hadn't lost that social power. This was the case in Germany before WWII, when Nazi organizers could reasonably ask their fellow Germans if their lives were better now under the Weimar Republic than they had been under the German Empire. The power of that message is still visible in the United States and the rest of the world today.

Before and just after the election of Donald Trump to the presidency of the United States in 2016, the far-right was more visible and powerful than it had been for several decades, at least since the time of the KKK's power during the Civil Rights Era in the US South. Openly right-wing figures like Richard Spencer and others edged closer and closer to openly calling themselves fascists. This political formation called itself the "alt-right," as in the alternative right. They tried to make themselves into a normal, expected part of the Republican Party, and came very close.

Then they held a rally in Charlottesville on August 11, 2017. At this rally, they marched with torches, screaming about their fears of being socially "replaced," a common fascist slogan about white people's worries of no longer being the most powerful group in our society. They mimicked Nazi marches and symbols, and one of their members killed a counterprotester, a woman named Heather Heyer, who had felt morally obligated to counterprotest this fascist rally.

This "Unite the Right" rally did anything but that. Instead, it sowed serious disagreement among the people on the right-wing about how to best organize and take power. Some thought that the right thing to do was to dive back into military-style terrorist organizations and organize themselves as insurgents, prepared to fight against the US Army, the National Guard, and the FBI. These groups were often small and dedicated and held trainings in rural areas, trying to prepare their members for armed insurgency against the United States or for inciting the kind of mob violence that they could take advantage of.

Others took a different approach. They continued to organize on the street while denying that they had wider political ambitions. Another strain of right-wing ideology that developed in the late 20th century was anti-government extremism. Based in an extreme form of libertarianism, these militants seek complete independence from all government control—either because they simply don't trust the government or because they think that it is part of some kind of malevolent plot to take over the world. Many of them move out to isolated, rural areas looking to escape the power of the government over their lives, primarily in terms of paying taxes and educating their children. This strain of far-right ideology is connected to some of the most violent acts of terrorism committed on US soil, including those of the Unabomber and Timothy McVeigh. McVeigh, in particular, was motivated by his hatred and distrust of the US federal government, targeting a government office in Oklahoma City. By the 2000s, anti-government extremism merged with the rest of the right-wing.

Some of the most worrying fascist organizations in the United States today are the Proud Boys and the Groypers. There are others—like the Three Percenters or the Oath Keepers—but they tend to recruit from older men, particularly veterans. The Proud Boys and Groypers, conversely, are mostly made up of younger men, mostly white, who look around and see that the world is getting less easy for them—they're losing power relative to other people in our society. They want to fight this decline in their social power, and they're willing to do whatever is necessary for that fight. This means anything from supporting right-wing candidates in political activity to engaging in street violence to helping Donald Trump try to overthrow the government of the United States.

The Proud Boys are a fascist street gang started by influencer and media personality Gavin McInnes, who was also a founder of VICE Media and one of the original Millennial "hipster" tastemakers in Brooklyn in the 2010s. McInnes was with a group of friends in Manhattan, having just seen the Broadway adaptation of the Disney movie "Aladdin," when they started a conversation about one of the songs in the show, "Proud of Your Boy." The song has Aladdin wishfully hoping that he might do something that will make his mother proud of him.[10]

McInnes mused to the group he was with that men shouldn't need to rely on others being proud of them; that they should be proud of themselves just for being men—and that's where the idea for forming the Proud Boys came from. As a group, the Proud Boys engage in openly gang-like activities. They start fights on purpose, hoping to prove their masculinity. They have violent hazing rituals, with people only allowed to be full members of the group if they've been assaulted by the other people in their local circle. They have a uniform based on white nationalist wear in the United Kingdom: black polo shirts with bright yellow accents (yellow has often been the color of fascism), with the buttons fastened all the way up.

Like most fascists since 1945, the Proud Boys don't use the word "fascist" to describe themselves—although they sometimes flirt with some openly fascist symbols, like the Nazi salute. Instead, they call themselves "Western chauvinists." By "Western," they mean "the Western world," a controversial term that can sometimes just mean the United States and Europe, but often carries racial and ethnic connotations. When they talk about defending "Western civilization," they mean some particular things—they mean whiteness, and the claim that white people developed, in their view, "everything good in the world," from science to music to democracy. They also mean Christian, another dog-whistle use of the word "Western" that harkens right back to the ways that fascists in the 20th century talked about Europe as being the homeland of white people, only "invaded" by Jewish people.

While the Proud Boys don't use language that is explicitly racist and even have many leaders who are people of color, their politics still follows the same logic that would be used to exclude or discriminate against people of color. Their claim is that Western civilization is the best—hence their "chauvinism"—that they won't apologize for it being better than other cultures, and that it's their job to protect it from its enemies. Those enemies are the left, queer people, and, implicitly, Jewish people.

Since their founding in 2016, the Proud Boys have been involved in fascist violence at various levels in the US political system. They've run "security" for local politicians in Oregon and elsewhere. They've attended the same galas as GOP establishment conservative leaders like Ann Coulter, except that they get into literal fistfights on their way into the building. They've held marches and rallies, which are explicit attempts to get leftists to fight with them. Sometimes they end up fighting the police, but more often than not, they end up fighting leftists and anarchists who show up to their rallies explicitly to prevent them from taking up space without being confronted. They received a major morale and publicity boost in the 2020 US presidential election when Joe Biden asked that Trump denounce them and other fascist groups. Instead, Trump only told them to "stand back and stand by," which they interpreted as an endorsement and a call for them to hold their power in reserve for a more dangerous time—which is exactly what they did.

The Proud Boys were instrumental in Donald Trump's attempted coup on January 6, 2021. Their leader at the time, a man named Enrique Tarrio, was in DC for the rally (although he couldn't participate as he was blocked from entering DC due to a previous right-wing militant act involving him burning a Black Lives Matter banner at a historically Black church). Members of the Proud Boys left President Trump's rally early to pave the way for the other protesters to invade the

Capitol building, operating as a right-wing paramilitary prepared to fight police and the National Guard in order to aid their chosen political leader. Tarrio and many of the other Proud Boys have since been convicted of seditious conspiracy and have received long jail sentences.

Since January 6, the Proud Boys have been a much smaller and less influential force, partly due to the legal troubles they've found themselves in now that their leaders are being held for criminal charges related to their crimes. There's even good reason to believe that their leader, Tarrio, is cooperating with the FBI and other investigators. Many of their leaders, including Tarrio, have already been convicted of serious crimes related to Trump's attempted coup on January 6, 2021. At a national level, this means that the Proud Boys are not doing well—but at a local level, some chapters are still going very strong.

Other fascist paramilitaries and street gangs have taken their place, such as the Patriot Front. Openly wearing fascist symbols and proudly posting videos of their paramilitary training online, the Patriot Front is the clearest imitation of 1920s and 30s-style fascist organizations in the United States today.

The other major group of fascists that appeal to young people in the United States is the Groypers. Not a paramilitary or gang, the Groypers are a network and political movement centered on the right-wing influencer Nick Fuentes. The name for the collective comes from a meme that depicts a large green frog—a variant of the "Pepe the Frog" memes that were more popular as symbols for the alt-right from 2015 to 2017, during the height of the Trump campaign and the first years of his administration.

Fuentes hosts the popular America First show online, in which he appears dressed in a suit and tie with a fake NYC skyline backdrop, mimicking a right-wing talk show like Tucker Carlson or Bill O'Reilly. Unlike those personalities, who generally hide their clearly racist, sexist, anti-queer, and anti-immigrant messages behind smokescreens and dog whistles, Nick Fuentes is brazen with his bigotry. He openly calls for violence against women, people of color, Jewish people, queer people, trans people, and many others whom he considers to be less worthy and less American than he is.

Most important for Fuentes's brand is that he is a young "incel." Incel is a portmanteau of the words "involuntary" and "celibate," and they're part of a wider rallying cry for young men against women that I'll give further details about in Chapter 2. Fuentes uses his position as an incel to connect with down-and-out young men who, arguably correctly, think that their position in the world is on the decline.

Fuentes also runs the influential America First Political Action Committee (AFPAC). AFPAC presents itself as a right-wing response to CPAC, the Conservative Political Action Committee, which is the largest and most important gathering of conservative voices in the United States and has been since 2020. Far from the fringe meetings that the openly fascist alt-right presided over earlier, AFPAC gets big names in the GOP to attend its rallies, people with actual power in the real world, like US Representatives Paul Gosar and Marjorie Taylor Greene.

As I write this section, the 2024 election in the United States has just concluded with another victory for Donald Trump. His promises are arguably more extremist than they were in 2016. What this means for the future of fascism in the United States remains to be seen, but their power and influence aren't going away anytime soon.

Fascists Outside the United States

These examples are some of the worst right-wing movements in the United States; the recent trend of right-wing resurgence isn't isolated to the United States. It's a global one that must be understood as covering the whole world.

In Spain, the VOX party has exploded on the national scene and won significant levels of support. VOX takes its cues from Spain's fascist history while maintaining the appearance of a normal parliamentary party. Like most other right-wing parties that are trying to capitalize on the resurgence of fascism, they don't use fascist slogans or images and instead focus on mainstream acceptance. VOX is led by Santiago Abascal, who has been making a name for himself on the international extreme right-wing by appearing at rallies and events led by other right-wingers. Even more extreme than him is Lius Peréz, an online influencer whose party, called "Se Acabó la Fiesta" (The Party's Over), recently won a handful of seats representing Spain in the EU Parliament in a 2024 election.

In France, the National Rally has long been a major contender for political power. Founded in 1972 by Jean-Marie Le Pen, the National Front (renamed the National Rally in 2018) has contested parliamentary and presidential elections for decades. It received its first national success in 2002 when Le Pen made it to the second round of the French presidential election for the first time. Since then, he and today his daughter and political successor, Marine Le Pen, have contested every presidential election, often doing very well, coming in second place on two more occasions. Their party has become a mainstay of French politics, even as scandal after scandal revealed Le Pen's connections with anti-Semitic propaganda, their disdain for non-white French citizens, and their association with more radical right-wing groups. As I write in late 2024, the party is led by Jordan Bardella, an under-30 radical right-winger representing the future of French right-wing politics.

In the United Kingdom, the most recent major success of the UK right was the Brexit vote, which dovetailed perfectly with right-wing nationalist politics. The Brexit campaign was spearheaded by a now-defunct political party called UKIP, the UK Independence Party, led by Nigel Farage. Since then, Farage has become a floating member of the international right, appearing as a speaker in the United States and elsewhere. In the 2024 parliamentary election, he returned to electoral politics as the leader of the far-right Reform Party. Another important figure in the United Kingdom far right is Stephen Yaxley-Lennon, aka Tommy Robinson, founder of a gang of street thugs called the English Defense League that mixed football hooliganism with anti-Islamic racism. Andrew Tate, the discredited male chauvinist influencer who has been accused of human trafficking and rape, is also a UK national.

In Italy, the right-wing has come back to power via a party that is literally descended from the Italian Fascist Party. This group, led by Giorgia Meloni, has ridden on the coattails of decades of conservative power led by Silvio Berlusconi, who was a junior member of their political coalition. Meloni has already put Italy on a path toward a more nationalist political footing by opposing queer rights, attacking immigrants, and honoring her country's fascist past. She has become a major proponent of right-wing political issues not just in Italy but in Europe as a whole. Her party has a large youth wing, of which she was previously a leader. Its explicit goal is to grow her party and movement by getting more young people interested in the far right-wing.

In Germany, the far-right party Alternative for Germany (AfD) has been on the rise since its foundation in 2013. Most successful in the parts of Germany that were once behind the Iron Curtain, the AfD originally presented itself as an anti-immigration party and a "Eurosceptic" party, meaning that it opposes free migration within the European Union and is critical of the EU's governance. Since its foundation, however, the AfD has been moving further on the political right-wing, engaging in open nationalism and racism that had been unthinkable in German politics since the conclusion of WWII and the downfall of the Nazi Party. It is also known for its connections to more openly extremist organizations, and for propaganda campaigns that just barely fail to meet Germany's postwar censorship laws, which prevent the depiction of Nazi-like images in political contexts. As I write this in 2024, the AfD has been extremely successful in recruiting young men to vote for them and to join their political ranks, using online appeals that focus on traditional values and the sense of deprivation young men have when they are single.

In Brazil, the far right-wing had its greatest success since the 20th-century military dictatorship in the election of Jair Bolsonaro to the presidency. Himself a former member of the military government, Bolsonaro spent decades as a vocal but minor opposition figure in the Brazilian Congress leading up to his surprise presidential victory in 2018. During his four-year term, Bolsonaro presided over the greatest level of deforestation the Amazon has ever experienced, a massive wave of misogynist violence that he considered to be a joke rather than a threat to national stability, and two genocidal policies—one toward indigenous peoples in the Brazilian north, and another in the form of his complete rejection of all COVID-19 precautions and policies. Bolsonaro used his connections in the Brazilian military and police to attempt a coup during his reelection campaign, arranging for members of the Brazilian highway police (which are part of the military in Brazil) to blockade strategically chosen highways in the country to reduce potential votes for his opponent, Lula. This failed, and to avoid prosecution, Bolsonaro fled to the United States, where he remained until March 2023. Bolsonaro is now under criminal prosecution for his involvement in these coups and for a series of corruption and money laundering scandals.

In Hungary, the right-wing has held power for nearly a decade in the form of the Viktor Orban government. Orban represents the Fidesz Party, which began as a mainstream conservative party but has since become increasingly right-wing. This is in part due to the strong opposition he's faced from what was an even more right-wing, almost openly fascist party called Fidesc. To protect his right flank, Orban has moved his own party further and further right and has become an almost openly fascist party itself.

In India, the ruling BJP is part of an umbrella organization called the RSS, a Hindu nationalist movement that began under British colonial rule and has since continued to develop a strong right-wing response to India's cosmopolitan society. A member of the RSS was one of Indian independence leader Mohandas Gandhi's assassins, and the RSS sponsors memorial vigils for this assassin rather than for Gandhi. For decades, the RSS paraded in uniforms and trained its members in para-military activity primarily directed against Muslims and other non-Hindu groups in India. They've also been an important force behind the development of an increasingly powerful and exclusionary Hindu nationalist identity in India, one that claims that Islam is a foreign presence in their country that needs to be expelled by force. While the RSS has moderated somewhat in the last few decades, it and the BJP have only become more popular as the representatives of right-wing Hindu nationalism. India, like most countries, also has a robust crop of right-wing influencers who mix fitness and dating advice with conservative political messaging—some examples include Sandeep Maheshwari and Khan Sir.

By the time you read this book, it's possible that some, or all, of these people will have been eclipsed by some new group, a new leader, or some new way of organizing. That means that instead of focusing on these particular people, you should focus on the movement they represent and the threat they pose to your son and your community.

I've shared these examples to show that wherever you are, in whatever country you're reading this book, the right-wing likely has a decided presence around you. Even if you think that your country is immune to the dangers of the right-wing, that it "can't happen here," remember that the people in Germany, Italy, Spain, and Romania thought the same thing in the 1930s and 40s.

These groups, though, are only the very vocal and outward-facing part of a large and hard-to-define group of people. Most fascists aren't members of particular organizations, don't attend meetings or pay dues, don't wear uniforms or turn up to rallies. Just like with almost every other political ideology, most people stay at home and live out their beliefs in their conversations with friends and family. This means that it often isn't easy to tell when someone is getting interested in fascism, because it'll be more subtle. The jokes they're interested in might change, or the people and celebrities they admire. Their friend groups might change, but probably not wholesale.

Most of the time, when a young person starts to flirt with the right-wing, it won't be sudden. They might maintain some friendships with people they disagree with. Homophobic people might stay friendly with gay people they know, or racists can have relationships with people of color. This cognitive dissonance, when people say one thing and do another, is normal and, in fact, is a hopeful sign that they aren't so far gone that they have completely reoriented their lives around their newfound beliefs. Using these relationships is one way to talk someone down from a right-wing cliff, something I'll get into more fully in later chapters.

Reading this chapter, you should come away knowing two things—one, fascism is not new. It has over a hundred years of history across the Western world, with almost every country having one or more fascist organizations rise and fall throughout its history.

Two, fascism is not unusual. This might go without saying after emphasizing that fascism was everywhere in the early 20th century, but it's worth emphasizing. Fascism is a form of politics that existed, and still exists, almost everywhere in the world. These groups may be small, but they are everywhere. Once we accept that fascism isn't an anomaly but a common part of our political world, it's easier to accept that it can't be dismissed as just a phase or a fad when a young person gets attracted to it. Instead, it forces us to confront it as a real and disturbingly everyday part of our political world.

I don't mean that to be reassuring. Just because something is normal doesn't mean it should be accepted in our everyday lives. Instead, the fact that fascism and other expressions of the extreme right-wing are normal parts of most political worlds means that we have our work cut out for us if we want to stop the rise of the right-wing.

Notes

1 If you're interested in looking further into possible definitions of fascism, I suggest reading: Blinkhorn, Martin, *Fascists and Conservatives: The Radical Right and the Establishment in Twentieth-Century Europe*. London and Boston: Unwin Hyman, 1990; Griffin, Roger, *Fascism*. Oxford and New York: Oxford University Press, 1995; Müller, Jan-Werner, *Contesting Democracy: Political Ideas in Twentieth-Century Europe*. New Haven, CT: Yale University Press, 2011; Paxton, Robert O., "The Five Stages of Fascism," *The Journal of Modern History* 70, no. 1 (1998): 1–23.

2 Gonçalves, Leandro Pereira, and Caldeira Neto, Odilon, *O fascismo em camisas verdes: Do integralismo ao neointegralismo*. 1ạ edição. Rio de Janeiro and Brasil: FGV Editora, 2020.

3 If you're curious, you can check out Levy, Carl, "Fascism, National Socialism and Conservatives in Europe, 1914–1945: Issues for Comparativists," *Contemporary European History* 8, no. 1 (1999): 97–126; Müller, Jan-Werner, *Contesting Democracy: Political Ideas in Twentieth-Century Europe*. New Haven, CT: Yale University Press, 2011.

4 Trump's allies and surrogates, such as Roger Stone, are known to have met with people who participated in the insurrection. Mosk, Matthew, Rubin, Olivia, Dukakis, Ali, and

Gallagher, Fergal, "Video Surfaces Showing Trump Ally Roger Stone Flanked by Oath Keepers on Morning of January 6," *ABC News*, February 5, 2021. https://abcnews.go.com/ US/video-surfaces-showing-trump-ally-roger-stone-flanked/story?id=75706765.
5 De Meneses, Filipe Ribeiro, *Salazar: A Political Biography*. New York: Enigma Books, 2009; Laqueur, Walter, Mosse, George L., and Allardyce, Gilbert, *International Fascism, 1920–1945*. New York: Harper & Row, 1966; Levine, Robert M., Columbia University, and Institute of Latin American Studies, *The Vargas Regime; the Critical Years, 1934–1938*. New York: Columbia University Press, 1970; Pinto, António Costa, *The Blue Shirts: Portuguese Fascists and the New State*. Boulder, CO and New York: Social Science Monographs; Distributed by Columbia University Press, 2000.
6 Siemens, Daniel, and Burnett, David, *The Making of a Nazi Hero: The Murder and Myth of Horst Wessel*. London: I.B. Tauris, 2012.
7 The SA was the first paramilitary wing of the Nazi Party, it would later be replaced by the SS. See Peukert, Detlev, and Deveson, Richard, *The Weimar Republic: The Crisis of Classical Modernity*. London: Allen Lane, 1991.
8 The most famous of these accounts is: Putnam, Robert D., *Bowling Alone: The Collapse and Revival of American Community*. New York: Simon & Schuster, 2000.
9 McAleer, Tony, *The Cure for Hate: A Former White Supremacist's Journey from Violent Extremism to Radical Compassion*. Vancouver, BC: Arsenal Pulp Press, 2019. Pg 48.
10 This song and the character of Aladdin's mother were cut from the 1992 Disney movie but included in the Broadway production.

2

WHY YOUNG MEN?

I have a friend who's worked in secondary education for several years. When I asked him about how he sees masculinity and masculine fragility show up in his work with young men, he answered: "This year [2022]," he said, "more than one teacher has come up to me in my capacity as a discipline administrator to talk about students discussing and citing Andrew Tate. This wasn't surprising, but it was alarming."

For those of you fortunate enough to not be familiar with Tate, allow me to be the bearer of bad news. Andrew Tate was a moderately successful professional kickboxer in the early 2000s until his retirement in the 2010s. Afterward, he pivoted to work as an online influencer and operator of several online businesses, including a get-rich-quick scheme "online university," a webcam service featuring stereotypically attractive young women, and videos prominently featuring his aggressive hypermasculinity. These videos and services were wildly popular among young men from the late 2010s to 2022, when Tate finally began to face the consequences of his actions.

In December 2022, Andrew Tate was arrested in Romania and accused of operating an international human trafficking network that kidnapped women and forced them into sexual slavery. He'd set himself up in Romania to escape what he considered to be draconian consent laws in the United Kingdom. By the time my friend's students were talking about Tate, his crimes were a matter of public record. But that didn't stop them from identifying with him, sympathizing with his situation—being in jail for sex trafficking and rape—or from expressing agreement with his content, which pushed young men to devalue themselves if they weren't rich, physically strong, or socially domineering.

Continuing to discuss Tate, my friend went on: "Right-wing stuff has been a constant theme at school; young men just find it online. And the content has gotten

DOI: 10.4324/9781003385509-3

scarier as time has gone on." My friend teaches at a private preparatory school in a major metropolitan area. It has a diverse student body and teaches students social and emotional learning. It encourages students to do community service and has a restorative justice approach to discipline. None of this has stopped the students from encountering right-wing messaging or from spreading it on campus and in their private lives.

My friend has countless examples, each of them prefaced by him saying that he has just one more anecdote to share. Here's only one, dealing with sex and gender: "I had a 9th-grade student, very young. He was in a class I was teaching about science fiction and visions of the future. I asked the class what they thought of as the biggest problems facing our society, and he said that the biggest problem was the 'lack of traditional women.' I started to explain, as well as I could without him feeling punished, that I don't think describing women as 'traditional' or 'less traditional' is a good way to go. I just had no idea where he had gotten that from. In a different version of that class, years later, I was asking them to imagine different futures for the world—maybe futures where people didn't need to work for money to survive. A student raised his hand and asked if I was a communist—it was like I'd triggered something in him that he gave that response."

If you have a young man in your life, you probably aren't surprised by what my friend is saying. You might have heard your son say something like this or tell you that his friends are, or have heard that this is what young men are talking about. You might've heard them mention Andrew Tate or someone like him. Comments like these might be the reason you picked up this book in the first place. I wrote this chapter to get to the bottom of why young men are so susceptible to this kind of messaging.

This chapter will address these two central questions: **Why do fascists tend to recruit men?** And, **why do they tend to recruit young people?**

Fascism doesn't just appeal to young men because of its politics—there are also aspects of young men *themselves* that make them more susceptible to fascist messaging than young women and nonbinary children. Young men are more likely than any other demographic to participate in violent political activity of any kind.[1] Since fascism is a radical political movement, it needs young men to be on the ground participating in rallies, going to events, and becoming its new leaders, just like any other ideology.

More importantly for fascism than for other political movements, young men are also the most violent demographic, regardless of race or other dividing criteria, at last count committing 80% of the violent crimes in the United States.[2] Because of what we learned in the first chapter about how fascism uses violence to achieve its political goals, it should come as no surprise that fascists heavily recruit from this violent demographic.

Understanding the connection between right-wing violence and young men means focusing on the violence that right-wing men commit. In this chapter, I will tell you the stories of several young men who fell into the extreme right-wing and engaged in violence, usually based on misogyny. I'm telling you this ahead of time because these stories are disturbing and affecting, and you should be prepared when they come up. These stories are an important part of explaining fascist violence and fascist organizing, especially as they relate to sex and gender.

The Problem of Young Men

There's a whole universe of books today about the problems facing boys and young men. Some of them are directed at the young men themselves, others at their parents, and others at society as a whole. Many of these books are essentially conservative in nature. They assume that men are, in a word, "manly," in a Roger Moore or Ron Swanson sort of way. That comes with a lot of essentialist gender assumptions that I'm trying to avoid in this book, but which might be helpful for you to understand if your son is interested in the right-wing.

The thrust of most of these books is that there's a crisis in masculinity in the Western world. Most of these books agree that this crisis began in earnest in the 1970s, though some of them date it to earlier, even as far back as the 1800s. Whenever they decide it began, the sources agree—the problem is that society has "changed," and that what we consider men to be needs to change along with it. Michael Kimmel writes about these changes, arguing that "when men are incapable of living up to the ideals their culture has set for them" they experience an "aggrieved entitlement," a sense that the rules of the game have changed.[3]

These books will tell you that men and masculinity are stuck in older notions of what it means to be a man—that the central assumption of masculinity is that men are in charge of their families and their homes, that they are earners and workers rather than caregivers, and that they take up a large amount of public space and wield power. This version of masculinity is identified with my grandfathers' generation and the mid-20th century. They were loud, boisterous men who told ribald jokes and expected you to listen. They didn't cook or clean, even when they lived alone. They worked in factories, at laborious jobs, or ran a small business. They were Republicans or conservative Democrats. They left the feelings to their wives, and never once in my life did I see any of them cry, except about baseball or dogs.

But the assumptions of the world they grew up in no longer apply to our world. There's almost no working-class or entry-level job that can support an entire family with a single income, meaning that even if a man wanted to be just a breadwinner for his family, it would be nearly impossible for him to do it right out of high school or even college. This means that instead of providing for their families while women care for them, men share the role of financial provider with women but lag far behind women in terms of caring for their children, relatives, and themselves. The very definition of masculinity is in question for millions of people.

What's worse, according to many of these books, is that the traits associated with masculinity are also in question or already denied by society. Men are decisive and forceful, boisterous, even arrogant and violent—things that modern society generally frowns upon—unless the person in question is already powerful. But the issue is that there's a lack of alternate traits for men to take up as their own, distinct from women.

This is a legitimate social crisis. Lacking examples of male behavior that share the role of provider but also engage in caretaking, many men—and especially young men—are left without good models for themselves as partners, fathers, friends, or community members. Instead, the models they have for masculinity are increasingly harsh and even violent, directly tied to the resurgence of the right-wing.

The simple fact is that most fascists are men. Back in the first wave of fascism in the 1920s–40s, fascist parties were almost all founded and led by men. Many fascist groups also had what were called "female auxiliaries," side organizations led by and consisting only of women, but they were subordinate to the male-led central party.[4] This continues to this day: the Proud Boys in the United States, the RSS in India, and many other groups are either dominated by men or exclusively male. Surveys show that in the United States, young men are becoming more conservative at a vastly greater rate than young women.[5]

To understand why fascist groups are so dominated by men, it's helpful to understand what they themselves say about gender. Essentially, fascists argue that society at large has become weak and effeminate due either to their being subordinated to an outside force or to the success of previous generations in keeping our current one safe.

Usually, the outside force that fascists think their society has come to serve is some kind of international feminist conspiracy. I'll talk more about fascism and feminism in a moment, but as an introduction, the fascist position is that feminism is a tool of the Marxist left whose goal is to socially subordinate men to women and to produce a feminized or androgynous society. They think that moves to criminalize or even simply call out sexist behavior are forms of oppression against "real" men who naturally want to control their families as little kings. They also argue that as big Western economies move away from manufacturing and blue-collar work, men have less place and power in society, and that this move isn't just the economy shifting because of changes in the world market but instead a vast conspiracy planned by secretive international forces. If this sounds familiar to how I explained antisemitism, that's because it is—in the minds of fascists, this is one big conspiracy.

To explain this decline, fascists also often invoke one of their favorite narratives, lifted from old-fashioned histories of the fall of the Roman Empire. They will say something along the lines of: "Hard times create strong men, strong men create good times, good times create weak men, and weak men create hard times." This quote comes from a post-apocalyptic novel and has weaseled its way into the popular imagination.

You might've heard this phrase before on social media, perhaps accompanied by an image of a broken ancient statue, a Viking warrior, or some other supposedly masculine symbol. If you haven't, ask your son if he has.

The idea behind the quote is that traditional masculinity—that is, violent protectiveness and the control of others—produces better and safer societies in which people can flourish and develop at their own leisure. Usually, when fascists talk about this today, the "strong men" they're talking about are from the early and mid-20th century, people like lumberjacks, Frank Sinatra, and Vito Corleone. They think that these men are the epitome of physical and personal strength and that they built a good world for themselves and their families (never mind that that world was based on racism, Jim Crow, colonialism, etc.).

In their minds, something went wrong starting in the 1960s. Men and women began to mix in ways they hadn't before. The family structure fractured with easier divorces, the birth control pill, and the legalization of abortion. People were no longer in physical danger, so they let their guard down and became less likely to defend themselves. As a reminder, this narrative ignores the racial dangers faced by people of color, the dangers of the Cold War, domestic and workplace violence, sexual violence, etc. The right-wing is only concerned with the kind of violence that "real men" encounter, like conflict over women and open warfare.

The fascists think that this produced generations of men who weren't raised by men but were instead raised by women or the state—generations of emasculated men who aren't violent, aren't controlling, and aren't powerful. And they believe that without such men, society has fallen into disorder and anarchy. That's why fascists praise violence and think that it's good for the world. They think it makes men stronger, and they believe that is the foundation of a good society. If you want a shorthand for this right-wing perspective, watch the movie *Fight Club*—fascists and the right-wing love this movie and take its satirical diagnosis of masculine problems at face value.

In other words, fascists argue that what they understand as masculine virtues are necessary for the existence of contemporary society itself. Because fascists think that the lack of strong men is the cause of our social disease, they also think men are the primary cure.

Right-wing figures and influencers have been making millions of dollars exploiting masculinity panic for decades. Sometimes these schemes make headlines and news stories, such as when Tucker Carlson, a prominent right-wing talking head and former Fox News host, featured a segment on the need for men to tan their testicles in order to improve the level of testosterone in their bodies.

Men's advocates are obsessed with how much testosterone is in men's bodies, to the extent that it becomes a pseudoscientific measure of a person's masculinity, just one example of how right-wing influencers use masculinity panic to make a buck. However they phrase it, the purpose of these claims is to make some men feel inadequate and not masculine enough due to a simple chemical balance inside their bodies, something they aren't responsible for and which has nothing to do with how masculine they are.

This singular obsession with testosterone leads right-wing and fascist sources to suggest unhealthy courses of action for young men, both mentally and physically.

Some right-wing sources go so far as to encourage all men to take testosterone supplements, whether or not they've been prescribed them by a doctor. Others suggest taking different "medicines" and compounds that they claim will enhance the body's own production of the hormone. The right-wing ideologue and huckster Alex Jones has made millions of dollars off this and similar schemes.

Their obsession with testosterone is combined with a fear of estrogen, a hormone that is associated with feminine development. Right-wing and masculinity panic influencers argue that an overabundance of estrogens in food has led to a decline in masculinity in the West. They particularly associate this with the rise of soy-based foods, particularly meat and milk replacements.

Studies have shown that this is all completely nonsense—the estrogen present in soy products has nothing to do with the estrogen in the human body and is only called that due to some incidental chemical properties that are unrelated to its function as a hormone.[6] Still, this hasn't stopped the right-wing and others who share their obsession with masculinity from claiming that the consumption of soy-based foods produces a complacent, docile, and emasculated population. This has led to a popular insult for non-conservative men, calling them "soy boys." In the right-wing imagination, "soy boys" have had their body chemistry altered by food and food additives, making them less masculine and less capable of the kind of interpersonal and political violence that the fascists demand of men. They connect the consumption of soy to left-wing politics, interpersonal softness, and emotional vulnerability.

Another mainstream way this manifests is in the right-wing obsession with fitness and especially muscular male physiques. This can be seen in everything from the association of hyper-masculinity with gym culture to calls from fascists to solve problems by weightlifting—a popular meme on the right-wing calls for young men who are socially lost or who have low self-esteem to "just lift, bro." Claiming that men's emotional problems and difficulties can be solved with physical activity rather than therapy or emotional honesty is a common and mistaken perspective, not unique to the right-wing, but for the right, it takes on a new and greater importance.

Many right-wing influencers focus on fitness and health advice as ways to get at young men. These strategies prey on young men's desire to be more stereotypically masculine and on general social assumptions about what it takes to be a man. Talking to young men in this way, trying to make them feel as if they're inadequate unless they do the right, manly thing, allows fascists to present their views and habits as if they're the obvious answers.

In recent years, a new form of fascist and neo-Nazi organizing has intentionally mixed racial hatred with fitness. Called "Active Clubs," these groups are disorganized cells of young men who combine white supremacist rhetoric and propaganda with martial arts and other physical training. Founded by Robert Rundo after the Unite the 2017 Right Rally in Charlottesville, the network of Active Clubs aims to be decentralized so as to avoid disruption by law enforcement while presenting itself as a harmless, apolitical group focused on male fitness and self-improvement.[7]

The right-wing has been obsessed with male fitness for a long time. Many fascist parties in the 1920s and 1930s started fitness clubs, focusing on bodybuilding and bodyweight training they thought would help men become better soldiers and better leaders. Their obsession with male bodies and bodily health tied directly into their belief that one could tell if a person was fit to be a leader based on the size of their head or other physical measurements. The right-wing also played an instrumental role in promoting camping and spending time outdoors as a cure for the problems of city living. The Boy Scouts themselves were founded by British colonial general Robert Baden-Powell, who developed a taste for the outdoors while oppressing African people in British colonies.[8] Baden-Powell believed that urban life was robbing young men of the opportunity to be "real men," which he thought required knowing how to start a fire, kill an animal, and survive in the wilderness.

Today, many right-wing influencers use this same panic over masculinity to recruit more young men and make money off their followers. Examples include Andrew Tate's "Hustler's University" and Alex Jones's online stores on InfoWars. These networks and organizations intentionally play off gender-based fears held by many men in Western society that they're not masculine enough—masculinity in this case understood as being physically powerful and intimidating, and conforming to standard gender roles that show desirable men to be muscle-bound. This is one of the newer models of right-wing organization, especially in the United States. So-called active clubs appear from the outside to be fitness groups or martial arts organizations, but, from the inside, are transparently right-wing groups that prey on men's sense of inadequacy.

Of course, this whole line of thinking is a sham. There are many ways to be a man that don't rely on physical power and dominance, and there are many people who aren't men who have those traits. There are men who are physically powerful but emotionally vulnerable and in need of support, and there are men who are physically weak but emotionally strong and resilient. But this kind of nuanced thinking is impossible for fascists.

Fascists and most on the right-wing would condemn these perspectives as "feminist," an intellectual death sentence in their circles. By feminism, they don't just mean the academic theories that come out of university campuses and Women's Studies departments. Nor do they just mean the actions of organizations like the National Organization for Women. They also don't just mean movements like the Me Too movement, which encourage women who have been the victims of sexual violence and harassment to speak out and be open about their experiences and their victimizers.

For the right-wing, "feminism" is a catch-all term that covers everything from women entering the workforce to birth control to the "loss of the traditional family," to LGBTQ+ rights movements, to why particular women won't have sex with them. It's an umbrella that encompasses anything they don't like that has anything to do with sex or gender.

The right-wing talks about feminism as if it were something imposed on mainstream, everyday society from the outside and from the top down, a perversion of the natural order in which men would be the more powerful and influential of the genders. Pseudoscientific theories that claim that women are only naturally suited to have and raise children lead these members of the right to consider women who don't have children to be lesser and to think of women who don't want children as having something terribly wrong with them.

Fascists think that it's their job to turn back the clock to a time when "men were men." By this, they mean that they want to go back to a time when men had all the jobs, when men were in total control of their families, and when men had power over women. This is a *vital* part of their ideology and one of the most compelling means they have of recruiting young men today. German fascists wanted to go back to the gender politics that they imagined were normal in the Middle Ages or even earlier, for example. The Nazi state gave women medals for things like the number of children they bore, promoting the idea that their service to Germany deserved recognition but that it was primarily as the potential bearers of new Aryans that they should be celebrated.

Fascists and the right-wing believe that women—by which they mean cisgender women—aren't fit for anything except giving birth, raising children, and maintaining family structure. This separates them from mainstream conservatives, who don't openly support taking away women's right to vote or their ability to hold property, even as they continue to promote politics that remove reproductive choice from women's lives or that take away important protections for gender equality.

This is not a small difference. Fascists take right-wing politics to their final end, not just engaging in political mobilization that dehumanizes others but which literally robs certain people of their legal humanity.

Fascism and the right-wing use gender to target their violence. We can see this clearly in some of the most recent mass shootings in the United States and elsewhere. As a warning, the next section includes some examples of this gendered violence. I've included these both as a reminder of its seriousness and as a tribute to the people who were harmed by it.

Gender and Violence

One of the earliest instances of modern misogynist mass violence is the École Polytechnique Massacre in Montreal, Canada, an advanced engineering school associated with one of Quebec's most prestigious public universities. The killer's name was Marc Lépine.[9] Lépine had shown years of violence and verbal abuse and had been fired from multiple jobs for this behavior. In 1986, he applied for admission to the École Polytechnique but was denied.

Lépine attempted to apply again and then complained that his failure to be admitted to the program was the result of women taking engineering jobs from men. This perceived social and structural slight was mirrored in his personal life—Lépine wanted a girlfriend but was dismissive of and verbally abusive toward women to the point that no women wanted to spend time with him. Lépine's belief that he was entitled to social and personal outcomes, despite doing nothing to earn them, is common among male supremacists.

By 1989, Lépine felt that he had reached his breaking point. He'd entered and dropped out of several programs and had come to blame all his problems on women and feminism. After this string of personal failures, Lépine decided that he would take the issue into his own hands and commit an act of violence against "feminism," which he directly identified with women in the engineering program.

He planned his massacre for six months before committing it, first by deciding where he would commit his violence and then by legally purchasing an assault rifle (purchasing such a weapon became significantly more difficult in Canada after this attack). He spent some time at the École, apparently planning exactly where he would begin and continue his assault. On October 6, 1989, he entered the building and began his massacre.

Lépine started in an engineering classroom, where he lined up the male and female students separately. He told the 50 male students to leave—which they did—and then shot the nine women who were left in the class, killing six. After this first violent act, Lépine moved on to different sections of the building, shooting dozens of others and killing eight more women. Lépine killed no men, though he injured four. Eventually, Lépine turned his gun on himself, committing suicide.

Upon his death, Lépine was found to have a suicide note in his jacket that detailed the motivations for his actions. In it, he is clear that he was inspired to commit these acts not because of his economic situation or because of difficulties in his studies— he was motivated by his hatred of feminism and his distrust of women in secure or powerful positions, specifically what he considered to be the "opportunistic" nature of feminism, claiming that it let women have the best of both worlds. The letter closed with a list of nearly 20 women in Quebecois society whom he wished to see killed for what he considered to be their "feminist" politics and closed with a quote from Julius Caesar in Latin—specifically what he is claimed to have said when he crossed the border of Italy with his legion, beginning the civil war that would result in the end of the Roman Republic and the establishment of the Roman Empire. The phrase, "let a die be cast," has come to mean that a point of no return has been reached. Lépine believed, or at least hoped, that his actions would be the beginning of another civil war, one in which men turned on women both structurally and personally in order to reestablish the supremacy over them that he and others like him believed men deserve.

As arguably the first modern anti-feminist massacre, Lépine's actions have become a rallying cry for other male supremacist extremists and those who believe that feminism is ruining the chances of men to achieve what they want and need in life. Despite this, and despite Lépine's own direct claims to have been motivated by feminism and the success of women, some observers continue to argue that his actions were the result of mental illness or some physiological condition rather than the behavior of a person who earnestly believed something monstrous that motivated him to do something monstrous.

After the attack, the Canadian government changed its laws regarding the purchase of assault weapons to make such an attack harder to carry out in the future. Feminists and members of women's movements in Canada were also motivated by the attack to advocate for more attention to the increasingly virulent nature of the attack on women.

Lépine committed his murders in 1989, long before the dominance of internet culture or the appearance of many of the websites and influencers who are blamed for right-wing political violence today. His story should remind us that the right-wing might *use* sites like 4chan or apps like TikTok to organize, but it doesn't need them. And while his attack may have been the first of the modern misogynist attacks, it has not been the last.

The 2014 attacks in Santa Barbara, California, are some of the clearest gender-motivated shootings in the history of the Western world. The perpetrator, Elliot Rodger, was motivated by a gendered ideology that argues he and other men were deserving of women's affection and sexual interaction, and that their denial of this to him was not just an insult but a political attack. This particular flavor of misogyny, called the "incel" movement (a portmanteau of "involuntarily celibate"), expanded in the 2010s as an expression of online vitriol against women, and especially attractive women, for their refusal to be with men who thought they deserved them.

Rodger was a student at UC Santa Barbara and the son of a mixed-race couple, a white man and an Asian woman. Rodger's father was a wealthy elite, and Rodger understood his mother as having been a conquest of his father and a representation of his success in business and society. Rodger led a privileged life, receiving gifts, cars, and designer clothes from his family's wealth.

However, he wasn't happy or satisfied. Rodger believed that this social position and wealth meant that he deserved to be seen as superior to other people, that he should be treated with respect and honor, and that he should easily be able to win over the women he considered to be the most attractive to have sex with him simply because of his wealth, status, and good looks.

He found that this wasn't the case at college. Women ignored him, and other men thought he was a little creepy. Roger expressed these thoughts extensively in a blog and a YouTube channel, which mostly consisted of him staring at the camera and complaining about how unfair it was that he, a deserving young man, couldn't get the kind of girl he wanted. He complained that these women weren't just dating white men—whom Roger understood to be socially superior to him as a mixed-race man. They were dating *Black* men, which Roger saw as some kind of topsy-turvy social reversal and essentially a betrayal of all social norms. To paraphrase, he asked himself and the viewer: "If I've done everything right, have a nice car, lots of money, and reasonably good looks, why won't they date me? Or, specifically, why won't they have sex with me?"

Roger's rants over these supposed injustices escalated to the point that he began to discuss the revenge he wanted to take on his fellow students. From the women, he wanted revenge for their not being willing to sleep with him. From the men, he wanted revenge for their having "taken his place" and been with women he thought were his by right. These views dovetailed with a history of mental and developmental disorders that he had faced since his youth—Roger had been prescribed an antipsychotic medication but refused to take it.

His words became more and more violent until he reached a breaking point. He began this killing spree in his own apartment on the night of Friday, May 23, 2014. He waited for his two roommates to arrive home and stabbed them one after the other. He also killed a third man who arrived at their home by stabbing. It was after these murders that his misogynistic killing began in earnest.

Roger left his home and drove toward the "sorority row" of UC Santa Barbara. There, he sat alone in his car for 45 minutes, apparently working on his laptop. In fact, he was finalizing a video manifesto called "Elliot Rodger Retribution," which he uploaded to YouTube at 9:17 PM. The next minute, he sent out his text manifesto via email to his therapist, who contacted his parents, who contacted the police. But by then, it was already too late.

Roger arrived at the door of a sorority, Alpha Phi, and knocked on the door. When no one answered, he started shooting at people in the area. He killed two women and injured a third. He then left the sorority and started shooting at nearby coffee shops and restaurants, killing one man who was sitting and eating. Roger then got back in his car and started shooting at businesses and pedestrians, specifically targeting women—he shot a couple and a woman riding a bicycle. It was at this point he encountered his first police officer, whom he shot.

Then Roger continued driving through Santa Barbara, shooting and running into pedestrians, cyclists, and people on skateboards. After further gunfire with police, Roger was found dead in his car at 9:35 PM, having shot himself in the head. He had over five hundred rounds of ammunition in his car. Excluding himself, Roger had killed six people—his two roommates and their guest, a man at a restaurant, and two members of the sorority he had intentionally targeted. He injured 14 others, seven with gunfire and seven more by hitting them with his car.

Roger's acts inspired a major surge in misogynist, racist, and otherwise right-wing sentiment on the internet, especially on websites socially dominated by men and men's issues. Roger was hailed as an example of the "incel" who met his breaking point, who decided that he was going to take the power he had to correct what he perceived as the "injustices" of the world that had denied him sex with women he desired.

"Incels" frame their arguments using the same structure and logic that oppressed people do when they talk about police violence, sexism, racism, and homophobia. That's because "incels" believe that their social situation is *equally* unfair and unjust as these real structural injustices. Their worldview centers on and relies on seeing themselves as victims. As victims, they claim that their oppression is both individual—in that individual women reject them—and structural—in that society devalues them and their personhood.

Among "incels," Eliot Roger isn't just a hero—he's a "saint," known as "Saint Eliot," and lauded as the "Supreme Gentleman," a title he gave himself in one of his videos complaining about why women didn't like him but did date men he considered to be less respectable and desirable than himself. By the time of his attack, Roger's misogyny had developed to the point that he considered all women to be inferior and deserving of death. In various public posts and videos created before his massacre, he said that he believed it was his job to start a "war on women," and that the world would be better if he and other incels put "a majority of women in concentration camps" so that they could "starve to death." He fantasized about a future without women, in which men would be free to live their lives and develop human civilization, in his words, without thawing to "worry about the barbarity of sex and women."

This attitude isn't isolated or unique—it's a relatively common one in certain corners of the internet, where young men like Roger have long found a refuge for their misogynistic politics. On various apps and websites—starting with 4chan and Reddit and increasingly moving to private Discord servers—they've developed a unique vocabulary for describing the world as they see it. They themselves are "incels" or "betas," men whom they think society as a whole looks down on and devalues due to their appearance, social skills, or income. The men they both loathe and aspire to be are "Chads," men whose masculinity and ability to get women to sleep with them is natural and easy. "Incels" have a complex relationship with the masculinity of so-called Chads, as they both want to emulate and learn from them but also hate them and hold them responsible for their own failures to secure the kind of female attention they desire.

There is no such complexity when it comes to their attitude toward the women they desire but do not have. These women are "Stacys"—like Chad, a name ripped from a Beverly Hills 90210 script. "Incels" believe that Stacys are both impossibly beautiful and completely undeserving, coasting on their looks with a ticking clock that will render them undesirable as they age. They think that these women choose Chads for their looks and their swagger, rather than choosing based on income potential or how much the man "deserves" to have them. Try asking your son if he's heard these terms online or from friends.

This sense of collective deprivation and harm has produced among supposed "incels" a sense of community organized around wanting women's attention, doing nothing to make themselves desirable dating partners, and hating women because of it.

Roger's acts weren't isolated. They inspired a series of copycat and mimic planned attacks, some of which were carried out. One of these was the so-called Toronto Van Attack, committed by Alek Minassian of Canada. Minassian is the son of Armenian immigrants to Canada, and prior to his massacre, he had no history of mental illness screening or treatment and no criminal record whatsoever, though he was in a special education class in elementary school due to difficulty social-izing. He joined the Canadian military after high school only to leave after 16 days, before completing his training. He then briefly followed in his father's footsteps and worked as a software developer.

This relatively normal life trajectory aside, Minassian considered himself to be a failure—and he blamed his failure on the society he lived in. He posted regularly to Facebook and other online communities, identifying himself as an incel. One such post, the one he sent immediately before his massacre, specifically called out 4chan and Elliot Rodger as inspirations for his participation in the "Incel Rebel-lion" to "overthrow the Chads and Stacys." Minassian's post closed with "All hail the Supreme Gentleman Elliot Roger!"

Minassian sent that post on April 23, 2018. That afternoon, he got into a large van he'd rented and took it onto the sidewalk of a promenade in Toronto, Canada. He drove for several minutes on multiple sidewalks, killing 11 people and injuring 15 more. After the Canadian police arrived on the scene, he pulled a dark object from his back pocket and held it at a police officer, who warned Minassian that he was prepared to use lethal force. Minassian demanded that the officer "shoot him in the head." When the officer realized that Minassian was not holding a gun and was trying to commit suicide by police rather than face arrest, he holstered his weapon and apprehended Minassian with his baton. His attack lasted all of seven minutes.

These and other examples of misogynist violence are part of a movement whose goal is to weaponize the anger some young men feel toward women into a social control scheme that could transform the world. This directly connects fascist organ-izing to the concept of the "incel," and makes their personal complaint about their disappointment with their sex life into a political one about the nature of society.

Hearing about the crimes of these individuals is important for understanding the stakes of the so-called incel debate, but it isn't nearly enough on its own. So far, I've been talking about "incels" as a group, as a part of our society, and argu-ing against their ideology and perspectives. I hope you agree with me that their assumptions about gender, sex, and race are disgusting. But that won't help you talk to your son as an *individual* person dealing with the kind of social issues that "incels" address.

Like other right-wing ideologies, the "incel" movement is founded on a real problem—or at least a problem that's real for the people who are experiencing it. It *is* embarrassing and even hurtful to be a young man who wants to be in romantic or sexual relationships and find yourself unable to get the connection you're hop-ing for. Sometimes that embarrassment and emotional pain come from others, who shame or criticize men who don't meet our society's gendered standards of sexual and romantic experience. Other times, it comes from these young men themselves, who've internalized hurtful assumptions about themselves and others. No matter what the source—from their peers and society or from themselves—these stand-ards create real emotional pain for those who are caught up in them.

I want to be clear: this isn't conceding that "incels" are the victims they think themselves to be. Their demands for "access to sex," phrased in the same way that oppressed people demand access to means of social justice and betterment, aren't worthy of consideration. Instead, they're both victims *and* perpetrators of the harm that our society's gender norms cause. When I was in college, my feminist club had a saying: "the patriarchy hurts everyone—it just hurts women more." That means that we can't ignore that men are harmed both psychologically and physically by the gender norms of our society, but we also can't ignore the harms they do because they are also harmed.

This section is a warning about the worst possible consequences of your son falling down a right-wing, misogynist rabbit hole. It's much more likely that your son would encounter the ideas that motivated these killings and participate in more mundane forms of sexist violence, whether verbal or physical. Don't let the brutality of the attacks mentioned here make those everyday forms of violence more acceptable. The point is that they're all part of a *system* of violence that the right-wing supports and pushes for daily. Seeing that system for what it is will help you keep your son out of it.

Fascists and Sexuality

Fascists, and others on the extreme right, often claim that homosexuality is "degenerate" or "decadent." What they mean by "degenerate" is pretty straightforward—they think that there is something wrong with some people's sexual desires and that they should be punished or killed for them. It's the second term, "decadent," that needs some explanation.

As said in Chapter 1, fascists and others on the extreme right-wing think that the world is in a state of moral and political decline. Everything that liberals, progressives, and leftists want, fascists despise. They think that immigration is diluting the national bloodline. They consider homosexual marriage to be an abomination and an affront to their religion. Anything less than complete support for the police and armed forces is evidence that the person is a traitor. For many fascists and right-wing people in the United States, even small cultural and personal buying behaviors are evidence of social and moral decline, with things as innocuous as men wearing pink and people riding bicycles being linked to this social decline.

Fascists believe that the left, progressives, and even other less extreme conservatives are responsible for these changes, which they think will cause social catastrophes and disasters. They believe that the erosion of what they consider to be traditional values—everything from opposing interracial marriage to "Leave It to Beaver" and eating steaks for dinner—will mean the total collapse of Western civilization. This belief that society is weak and ready to fall at any minute is extremely important to fascists because it underpins their demands for what they think of as a "return" to a better way of living. Never mind that the traditional lifestyle they promote only existed for a small segment of the population, when it was real at all.

This is what fascists mean when they say that our society is "decadent." They think that we've gotten away from what should be our social priorities, which in their minds are the defense of social systems that benefit white people, Christians, and straight men. They use this word, "decadent," to connect their claims to the way that historians have talked about the decline and fall of other empires and civilizations before the United States and the Western world.

Fascists often claim that this social and moral decay is the result of changes in how Western society treats and raises young men. They say that in the past—usually either the 1950s or some unnamed time hundreds of years ago—"men were men." By this, they mean that men were more prone to violence, more socially powerful, and dominant in their families (which depended on them entirely due to sexism). They contrast this to the present and claim that men today are weak, that they question themselves, and have lost some inherent powerful quality that made them men.

This question of masculine identity and position isn't limited to fascists or even to the right-wing. Social and political commentators across the political spectrum have written many books on the plight and position of men as the Western world changes and the things that had once been the sole purview of men, such as work, the church, and government, are opened to women and others. This book is an example of these conversations, talking about how to make a place for men in the present.

It goes without saying that the men fascists are talking about are only cis men, that is, not trans men. Fascists and those on their right-wing believe that trans men are only women pretending to be men, and that they need to be corrected for this, prevented from pursuing their chosen gender, or even that they need to be punished for taking hormones. This means that it's precisely the only men who choose to pursue masculinity despite society's assumptions and prejudices that the right-wing thinks aren't really men and need to be stopped from becoming or being them.

None of this is to say that there is no connection between fascism and homosexuality. Scholars and casual observers have long pointed out the homoerotic nature of fascists' obsession with male power, masculinity, and sexuality. In fact, one of the leading Nazis when Hitler took power, a man named Ernst Roehm, was a well-known homosexual (though not "out" by today's standards). He and the other members of his inner circle were purged by Hitler shortly after they'd taken over Germany, partly due to their political power and partly due to verifiable rumors of their homosexuality.[10]

There was a relatively brief moment in the early days of the alt-right, the most recently dominant fascist movement in the United States, when trans and gender non-normative people were accepted as members of the right-wing. This period also coincided with the right-wing's greatest acceptance of queer people—though in this case they were mostly accepting of gay men in keeping with their misogyny. Some clear examples of this trend would include people like Milo Yiannopoulos, a right-wing youth personality and frequent campus speaker, who was at the beginning of his career an out gay man. Yiannopoulos has since claimed to have been "cured" of his sexuality through an anti-gay camp and has recently resurfaced as the temporary manager of Ye's abortive 2024 presidential campaign and a right-wing personality.[11]

Putting It Together: Fascism and Masculinity

At the core of the right-wing's interest in young men is the fact that they are vulnerable, uniquely vulnerable as men. The right-wing preys on their isolation, the fragility of their masculinity, and their knowledge that the success of progressive politics could mean a loss of status.

Young men are isolated. In the United States and many other developed countries, this is partly explained by the fact that people, in general, are more isolated now than they have been in centuries.[12] Young people's social worlds have shrunk over the last several decades, with teens, adolescents, and young people reporting fewer friendships and even fewer close ones. Increasingly lacking community outside of school, young people turn to other sources of belonging, largely online, where communities and perspectives tend to escalate in their specificity and radicalization.

Young men are particularly susceptible to this isolation because of how they're socialized to ignore or repress their emotions. With no socially acceptable outlet to express themselves, they turn to increasingly intense forms of expression, like violent sports, violent games, and potentially real-world physical violence. The right-wing preys on the isolation of young men to tell them that there *is* a community they belong to—it's the community of men. In these circles, uniting men based on their gender means emphasizing only the most stereotypical features of masculinity, namely its violence, its intensity, and its push to protect and thereby control others. Right-wing propaganda, from the past to the present, teaches young men that it's their job to protect people and control them and that the left is trying to take away that privilege and responsibility.

Masculinity is more fragile than femininity in the contemporary world. Femininity has gotten a lot more expansive over the last few decades, while our assumptions about men are still that they can't be gentle or caring. Gender expression is a complicated and intricate thing, different everywhere and for every person, but as a rule, the limits of normatively acceptable masculinity are very small. Men aren't expected to express their feelings. Their aesthetic options are limited, as are their opinions and tastes. This, of course, is true about women too. But it's generally accepted by most people who study gender roles that masculinity is more limited and vulnerable to accusations that it isn't really masculine at all—that it's, in a word, fragile.[13]

Masculine fragility is especially pronounced in young men, and not just because of the hurtful and direct nature of childhood and adolescent bullying. Young men are only just starting to develop their senses of self and are struggling to carve out their identities. This means that any identity they hold is simultaneously deeply felt and also very shallow—their bodies and minds are changing so rapidly that they have little time to get accustomed to one set of feelings before another takes its place. Adolescence is also the time when most people first begin to experience sexual desires, which connect directly with masculine norms of possession and control.

There is another reason that the masculine panic of young men is hard to deal with: the fact that when the right-wing tells young men that the left is trying to make them less powerful than their fathers and grandfathers were, it's telling the truth.

If the goal of any real leftist politics is to improve the lives of everyone in our society and to democratize our government and even our economy, then it's inevitable that doing so will mean a relative loss of power and privilege for those who were previously at the top of the hierarchy. In most of the world, that means men who belong to whatever the privileged racial, ethnic, or religious group is in that place. Even people who aren't leftists or liberals, such as those who consider themselves to be centrists or pragmatists, generally agree that one of our political goals should be to make our social centers of power more representative, diverse, and fairly chosen.

Put simply, this means a loss of power for men in society. That's a goal I and many other men share. But it can be a difficult sell to an adolescent who isn't old enough to understand the history of oppression these changes are supposed to address and whose personal experience is one of being controlled rather than being in control.

This is why I am writing this book with parents and other caretakers of young people in mind. You have a unique opportunity to intervene in the lives of the young men around you as mentors and guides. And after reading this book, you should have a better idea of what the warning signs are for right-wing radicalization.

While a young man might realistically know that he's moving in the direction of the right-wing—and may, in fact, be very vocal and proud of this—he won't be able to understand the dangers associated with that path. He won't know the history of the right-wing or be able to understand the real cost of that trajectory on his future. He won't be able to see the personal and professional connections he could lose from moving further to the right or the emotional cost it could have on the people he cares about. It's your job to provide that perspective so that he can see it from the outside.

This is why I shared the stories of misogynist violence earlier in this chapter. Your son might not know the dangers of moving his life in a misogynistic direction, or he might not understand that jokes about Andrew Tate or Elliot Rodger are in poor taste. It's your job to talk him off that ledge.

Star this conversation off by talking about your son's own experiences. Hopefully, as his parent, you've already shown yourself to be a person he can trust to talk to about sex, gender, and romance—if that's not the case, then you need to build that trust first. These topics can be difficult for anyone to talk about, let alone a young person with their parent.

Don't demand that he share everything all at once, assuming that he has some secret, deep-seated misogyny to hide. Start by asking questions about the people in his life and how he feels about them. Open up about crushes or romantic relationships you had in your past. Be upfront about how you felt then—maybe you felt alone, vulnerable, or like nobody would love or want you. Maybe you look back and think that some of the messaging of the "incel" movement would have sunk its teeth into you. The first and most important thing to do is to establish a relationship of trust and understanding with your son. He'll only be able and willing to open up to you if you show him that it's safe!

If your son is talking about sex and gender in a way that's worrying, it might be hard to start a conversation with him about it. This isn't just because teenagers and young people generally avoid talking to older folks about these things—since we're specifically talking about the experience of young men who would like to be sexually and romantically active but aren't, there's an added layer of embarrassment and shame on top of what they might go through when talking about sex or gender in any other context.

Through it all, you'll have to be careful to validate some of your son's feelings and experiences without accepting all of his conclusions. It's reasonable to feel embarrassed or even hurt that the people he wants to be with don't return his affections! That's a normal human experience that almost everyone goes through. It's even reasonable to think that the social norms we have about dating, male sexuality, and romance are unfair! It's also reasonable for your son to feel resentful, angry, and hurt about people who have rejected him! Again, that's a feeling that most of us can likely relate to, especially in our youth.

The line you need to make sure your son understands is that while he gets to have his feelings of hurt and even anger at his situation, he can't decide that the problems he's having with one woman are problems with all women or with women in general. That's the key line that "incels" and others who follow similar misogynist thinking cross, where they think that their woes come from women as a gender. Rather than blaming our society, which places undue stress and expectations on men and their sexuality, they come to blame those who are even worse affected by those experiences.

Combatting this perspective will be an uphill battle. Many sources, in and outside your home, will be pushing this worse perspective on your son, telling him that his problems would be solved if only women behaved the way they're "supposed" to. Given what he's heard and seen in our culture, this might be something difficult for him to understand—he's just learning gendered norms and expectations and is likely to have internalized the most simplistic and basic of them.

Fascism and Youth

So far, I've addressed the first question I raised in this chapter—why do fascists focus on recruiting young men? Answering that question has also shown us what the right-wing's relationship to gender and sexuality is in general and how it tends to use gender-based thinking not only to recruit its members but also to guide its actions.

But what about the second question—why do fascists recruit the youth in general? This question gets to the heart of why I'm writing this book and why I'm glad you're reading it. Fascists tend to target young people, which means that parents, educators, and others who are influential in the lives of youth have a special role to play in preventing that radicalization. You are on the front lines in the fight against fascism.

Fascists target young men for recruitment and essentially always have. Historically, the fascist parties of the early 20th century were obsessed with vigor, speed, and vitality, all traits associated with the young. They thought that young men represented the promise of the future, both figuratively and literally as future fathers, and were obsessed with male virility. The language in their speeches centered on the hope to build a new world full of new men who were adequate to its pace and its challenges. Mussolini's earliest writings on the movement that he hadn't yet named Fascism call out for "the young in years and spirit" to take up arms for the nation in order to defend and renew it.[14]

The central issue we have to grapple with when it comes to the appeal of the right-wing to the young is that for a certain group of young men, the right-wing is, in a word, cool. It's the current and expanding ideology and subculture for a lot of young people, especially those who live in areas where they aren't exposed to many alternatives. Chapter 3 will dive deeper into how exactly young men get radicalized, both online and in person.

Young people are often drawn to more radical ideologies than older people.[15] But the issue with the right-wing's approach to young people, especially young men, is that they treat them as fodder for their paramilitary and other militant wings. The right-wing needs young people not just because they are invested in a politics that emphasizes youth, but because they churn through the young in the course of their political action. They need young people to do dangerous activities that their older members aren't willing to engage in any longer. They also need young people to seem like a growing and vital part of the right-wing as a whole—one of the biggest strengths of the extreme right-wing is that they can seem like the new growth area for conservatism, as they're the sector of right-wing politics that isn't dominated by people from older generations. Fascists and other members of the radical right can push conservative parties like the Republicans further to the right by offering them opportunities for growth in membership.

Fascists' obsession with youth and the young was both theoretical and practical. They believed in the power of youth as the future of their movement and also relied on the youth for membership, especially when their movements were new themselves. This is especially true for the smaller and less successful fascist movements, the ones that don't end up in high school textbooks. These small groups of street-fighting young men needed new young bodies to fill their ranks, protect themselves from other militant groups, and commit acts of violence. It was always these young men who took on the physical risks of the movement, these young men who put their lives on the line for their ideology.

This has remained true up to the present day. It's very rare that the leaders of fascist movements put their lives on the line in the way they expect from their followers. Instead, they tend to lead from the sidelines or stay online entirely while promoting their ideology, expecting their followers to go out and do the dirty work for them. Fascists target young men because they *need* them to be frontline foot soldiers.

This means reconsidering the limits of who we think of as the "victims" of fascism. Certainly, those who experienced its violence are its victims, as are those it singles out for harassment and verbal abuse. The societies it takes over might also be thought of as its victims. But what about its young recruits? Where is the line between fascists we can and should vilify and its new members, people who have themselves been targeted by this ideology and bent to its goals? Can we blame a 12-year-old for being brought in by an ideology and propaganda campaign that is specifically designed to appeal to his still-developing mind and his still-developing sense of self and community? And what should we do with such a person if they've fallen into this trap?

There's a strain of progressive thinking that it's not the job of people who are victimized by one group to educate their oppressors about the oppression they're committing. For example, they would say it's not the job of Black people to educate white people about racism in the United States or the job of women to educate men about rape culture or sexism in the workplace. I broadly agree with this sentiment.

But the situation is different when we're dealing with young people, and especially young people who are in our care. In this case, we're not dealing with an anonymous person in a crowd but instead someone we know deeply and intimately, possibly from the day they were born. As parents, caretakers, and educators, we've signed up to help them on the road to adulthood and independence. Just as helping them navigate school, social pressures, and the job world is part of our job, it's our job to keep them away from dangerous ways of thinking. For the purposes of this book, we're setting what should hopefully be a fairly low bar—not being a fascist.

Intervening against fascist and right-wing radicalization when someone is young is among the best ways to prevent them from being radicalized in the future. The heart of the intervention strategy I lay out in this book is empathy. If you're dealing with a young man you already know and already care about, then you are uniquely capable of developing the kind of relationship with him that would enable you to intervene and de-radicalize him.

Unfortunately, I shouldn't have to tell any of you who already have young men in your life that it is sometimes—even often—difficult to direct their behavior away from harmful or risky things once they've set their minds on them. This is due to both the tendency of adolescents in general to push and explore boundaries that they lived under as children, and a result of our society's particular socialization of young men. As a whole, we encourage young men to act big and to express only the least subtle emotions, such as anger and ecstasy. This makes any conversation about the delicate questions involved in steering your son away from harmful politics very hard, and it means that for many young men these conversations sound like ways to get them to act less like men and more like women. That kind of rhetoric is common across the right-wing.

The central problem is that the empathy required to get someone out of a right-wing spiral is precisely the kind of emotional engagement that the more extreme right-wing condemns. Starting a conversation with a son who has developed an interest in a misogynistic influencer by asking him to have empathy for women might be exactly the wrong thing to do. Many of these influencers feature arguments and counter-arguments for their positions in their videos and podcasts—for example, Nick Fuentes often covers sarcastic versions of what people might say in response to his views. So if you try to condemn your son's new politics from the get-go, he might just find himself alienated and even more isolated from you as a result.

Another difficulty in helping a young man through this time in his life is that his brain simply works differently from the way yours does now. In *The Teenage Brain* by Amy Nutt and Frances Jensen, the authors tell us that teens' brains are in many ways still growing and forming. We all know this is the case when it comes to children—we see them learning to read and do math, and we understand that they can't keep it all in their heads. We know we need to remind them how to tie their shoes or that flour and sugar taste different.

We expect more of teenagers, and rightly so. Teens are expected to be able to take care of themselves and to keep track of their work at school or even an actual job. They might even be put in charge of other children. This, and the fact that they may appear to be fully grown, can fool us into treating them like adults. But they simply aren't.

The Teenage Brain reminds us that teenagers' brains deal with emotional and logical situations very differently than adults do. You might already have the impression that teens are more willing to take on risks than adults are, and you're right—their brains quite literally assess risk differently. They're more willing to take on higher odds and ignore the possibility of catastrophic failure. This isn't just because they're inexperienced or because they haven't yet learned an important lesson. It's because their brains themselves work differently and process risk with scientifically noticeable differences.

This means that when it comes to extremist activity, conspiratorial thinking, or risky behavior, your son isn't acting out just to mess with you. It's because he understands the risks of what he's doing very differently than you do. You have to remember that your son's brain is not finished developing when he's a young person—human brains don't stop developing until they're 25. This literally means he will have a difficult time dealing with systemic explanations for his personal problems—he's wired to believe that his experiences are his fault and the fault of his peers, rather than that they can be explained by social norms or societal problems.

Unfortunately, even an extremely successful conversation with your son about these issues won't necessarily change his mood or situation. Knowing that the pain you're experiencing comes from social situations that are out of your control can be demoralizing, especially for young people. The later sections of this book have suggestions for ways you can engage your son.

The facts laid out in this chapter explain why this book focuses on preventing the recruitment of young men to fascist organizations. Not only have young men always been the largest base of fascist recruitment, but they also commit the most violence and most often lead fascist organizations. This is partly just a result of fascist politics itself, which privileges men and their leadership, but it is more than that—fascism is founded on emotions and actions that our society codes as masculine. Fascism wants to be powerful. It wants to be heard, wants to be in charge, and openly claims to know better than everyone else. Fascists today want to return to a time when men had much more control over society than they do today, turning back the clock on gender and sexuality liberation as well as race relations. Fascists want to control spaces and people.

Above all else, fascists are, and want to be, violent. They value violent behavior and violent rhetoric. Since these behaviors are understood in our society to be masculine, fascism is also identified with masculinity.

Notes

1 Dier, Aleksandra, and Baldwin, Gretchin, *Masculinities and Violent Extremism.* International Peace Institute and UN Security Council Counter-Terrorism Committee Executive Directorate, June 2022.
2 This data comes from FBI crime statistics, which can be found at https://ucr.fbi.gov/crime-in-the-u.s/2012/crime-in-the-u.s.-2012/tables/42tabledatadecoverviewpdf/table_42_arrests_by_sex_2012.xls.
3 Kimmel, Michael S., *Healing from Hate: How Young Men Get Into-and Out of-Violent Extremism.* Oakland, CA: University of California Press, 2018. Pg 6.
4 For more on women in hate groups, see the work of Kathleen Blee, especially: Blee Kathleen, M., *Inside Organized Racism: Women in the Hate Movement.* Berkeley: University of California Press, 2002.
5 De Visé, Daniel, "High School Boys Are Trending Conservative," *The Hill,* July 31, 2023.
6 Reed, Katharine E., et al., "Neither Soy Nor Isoflavone Intake Affects Male Reproductive Hormones: An Expanded and Updated Meta-Analysis of Clinical Studies," *Reproductive Toxicology (Elmsford, N.Y.)* 100 (2021): 60–7.

7 McDonald, Broderick, "Active Clubs: A New Far-Right Threat to Democratic Elections," *Al Jazeera*, May 2, 2024.

8 Honeck, Mischa, "The Power of Innocence: Anglo-American Scouting and the Boyification of Empire," *Geschichte Und Gesellschaft* 42, no. 3 (2016): 441–66. www.jstor.org/stable/24891244.

9 If you want to read more about him and his life, see his mother's memoir: Lépine, Monique, and Gagné, Harold, *Aftermath: The Mother of Marc Lépine Tells the Story of Her Life Before and After the Montreal Massacre*. Toronto: Viking Canada, 2008.

10 For more on fascism and homosexuality, see: Theweleit, Klaus, *Male Fantasies*. Minneapolis: University of Minnesota Press, 1987.

11 Montgomery, Blake, "Mil Yiannopoulos Desperately Declares Himself 'Ex-Gay,' Says His New Mission Is Conversion Therapy," *The Daily Beast*, March 9, 2021.

12 US Surgeon General Vivek H Murthy, "Our Epidemic of loneliness and Isolation," 2023, www.hhs.gov/sites/default/files/surgeon-general-social-connection-advisory.pdf.

13 The concept of "masculine fragility" is both a popular term you might see shared and talked about on social media and something that academics debate. In addition to searching for the topic on your social media platform of choice, if you're looking for an academic perspective see Vandello, J. A., Wilkerson, M., Bosson, J. K., Wiernik, B. M., and Kosakowska-Berezecka, N., "Precarious Manhood and Men's Physical Health Around the World," *Psychology of Men & Masculinities* 24, no. 1 (2023): 1–15. https://doi.org/10.1037/men0000407; Connell, R. W., *Masculinities*. 2nd ed. London: Routledge, 2005.

14 Mussolini, Benito, "Audacia!" *Il Popolo d'Italia*, November 15, 1914, cited in Griffin, Roger, *Fascism*. Oxford and New York: Oxford University Press, 1995.

15 Wallner, Claudia, *The Contested Relationship Between Youth and Violent Extremism*. Royal United Services Institute, 2021.

3

ONLINE AND IN-PERSON RADICALIZATION

Payton Gendron was born on June 20, 2003, in Conklin, PA. He attended high school in rural New York, just over the Pennsylvania border, and then community college nearby. He was known as a quirky but quiet person to his fellow students and generally kept a low profile.

Like many young men during the COVID-19 pandemic, his life became increasingly online. He fell down the rabbit hole of hateful content, seeing more and more extremist messaging and participating in online forums like 4chan, a chaotic internet forum that hosts a huge amount of hateful online content, and the Daily Stormer, the largest English-language right-wing extremist community online. There he found people who not only talked about racism and extremism openly but actually idolized people who had gone on mass-killing sprees—people like Dylann Roof, Anders Breivik, and Brenton Tarrant. Gendron ate up these posts, and, apparently, at some point decided that he didn't just agree with their politics; he agreed with their tactics.

He decided he would commit his own mass shooting. At the time, he was 18 years old.

Gendron began to plan his massacre starting in 2022. His politics were founded in the so-called Great Replacement Theory, a neo-Nazi ideology that alleges that white people are being replaced as the majority in the United States and Western Europe in what they call a "white genocide." Gendron decided that he would do "his part" to keep this from happening.

He searched online for places near him that had large Black populations and decided on New York's second-largest city, Buffalo, some 200 miles away. He did some scouting missions there to decide on a potential target for his shooting and chose a supermarket in a part of the city predominantly populated by Black people. He also purchased several firearms, all of them legally, as well as body armor—this

DOI: 10.4324/9781003385509-4

despite the fact that he had been under investigation for a previous violent threat at his school. He wrote a manifesto and posted it online, having plagiarized most of it from earlier mass shooters.

On May 14, 2022, Gendron arrived at the Tops Friendly Market in Buffalo and immediately began shooting people. Gendron live-streamed his attack from a camera on his helmet, hoping that people would watch him kill his victims. Fortunately, the service he'd used to stream his massacre, Twitch, shut it off quickly. He shot four people in the parking lot. He shot at many more people in the store, but they barricaded themselves in the break room or hid inside the store's refrigerator, where his bullets were blocked by the food on display. At one point, Gendron pointed his gun at a white patron of the store but turned away, apologizing. All told, he killed ten people and injured three others. All of his victims were Black.

Only six minutes after he entered the store, the police were outside and talking to him. He allegedly put his gun up to his neck as if to kill himself but was talked down by the police, who arrested him. Since then, Gendron has been convicted of murder, domestic terrorism, and hate crimes by the state of New York and sentenced to 11 consecutive life sentences. Federal charges for terrorism and hate crimes are still pending.

At his trial, Gendron expressed remorse and regret for his actions and blamed them on the internet. He said that he thinks that if he had been less online—if he'd found a real-life community rather than 4chan or other online forums—he might not have fallen into the same rabbit hole that he did.[1]

My goal in this chapter is to provide you with a starting point for understanding how fascists and other right-wing extremists get their messaging in front of kids and how they use that messaging to grow their ranks. I'll profile some of the most dangerous and influential websites, apps, and personalities that are around as I write this—but I also want to give you some more generic information. That will help you if you're reading this book years later when these particular characters and communities are no longer the center of right-wing organizing, or if you're reading this book and dealing with right-wing radicalization in a language other than English or a place other than the United States, Canada, and the United Kingdom.

Hate Is Hard to Spot

Short of moving your family to a small compound in the woods with no internet access where your son would only encounter people you personally know aren't right-wing, you can't stop your son from being exposed to radicalizing messaging online or in person. You can limit the amount of this content that your son sees, and you can make sure that he sees it with supervision or with your outside perspective, but the fact is that he *will* see it.

And this isn't just because of how the internet works today, pushing content at users based on algorithms that decide their tastes and try to push content that might appeal to them based on what they've already consumed. It's because right-wing and even fascist messaging is everywhere.

It's in news broadcasts that try to find a "middle ground" or that allow all viewpoints to have their say. It's on the radio, especially if you live in a rural environment in the United States, where talk radio hosts have long been proponents of extreme right-wing sentiment on-air. It's on school campuses in the form of student groups, formal and informal. And, of course, no amount of parental controls or online censorship can keep your son from making friends and acquaintances with other young men who do have access to that content, who might share it with him.

So, since you can't outright stop this messaging from getting to your son, you need to know what it is, where it comes from, and what it's for so that you can do your best to counter it. I'll talk about how to counter it in the next chapter—for now, let's focus on these messages themselves.

The most important thing to know about right-wing messaging online and in-person is that it probably won't look openly fascist or even conservative at a glance. Most of it will look like the other content your son might consume already, such as posts or videos about cars, sports, and video games. Their titles or creators probably won't mention politics directly. Almost all of it will be designed to be fun, and especially to be funny. This is done on purpose. The people who make this content want to be sure that the kids consuming it, and you, their parents, have a hard time realizing just exactly what this content includes. By intentionally hiding their content in memes and other formats, they get their ideas into the minds of young men without anyone knowing better.

This means that your son getting associated with fascist ideas or right-wing messaging won't look like a movie where a young man becomes a skinhead, at least not at first—it'll look more like him falling down a media rabbit hole, getting obsessed with an internet celebrity you've never heard of, or starting to laugh at more off-color jokes than he used to. It might not change his friend group, since this kind of politics is so widespread in contemporary culture that he might not alienate his friends (unless his friends are women or nonbinary). Following these ideologies doesn't come with a uniform or a specific taste in music like subcultures did in the 90s and early 2000s. And most of it—in fact, the vast majority of it—is conducted in private, on cell phones and computers, hard to see and even harder to prevent.

So, given that your son will encounter this content, it's up to you to give yourself the skills and knowledge you need to counter it. You'll need to counsel your son on what he'll see and hear—or really, what he's already seeing and hearing. You'll need to keep your eye on warning signs, key phrases and behaviors, and to stay on top of online trends as they constantly change.

Video Games

There's been a lot of ink spilled over the dangers of right-wing radicalization via online or electronic sources. If, like me, you're old enough to remember some of the video game scares of the 1990s, you'll recall how the violent video games played by the Columbine shooters were used as an explanation for their violence. Pundits like Mary "Tipper" Gore argued that violent video games caused children to exhibit violent behaviors and pushed for their regulation. Since then, there have been dozens, if not hundreds, of books detailing how these new forms of media are shaping youth for the worse and leading them down dangerous paths.

When I say that video games are radicalizing youth, I don't mean to resurrect the ghost of video game moral panics from the past. These debates from the 1980s and 90s over violence found in many video games, for example, Mortal Kombat, sparked debate and public outcry that made its way to the US Congress in 1993, with both conservative and ostensibly liberal politicians arguing that these video games were going to transform the children who played them into violent thugs. This, of course, didn't happen—there's a good chance that you played video games while growing up, just like I did, and there's a good chance that some of them had violent content. Studies over the last several decades have shown that playing video games doesn't correlate to violent behavior, or any other kind of behavior for that matter.[2]

Video games themselves don't radicalize young men to the right-wing. Millions of people of all genders and ages play video games that are violent, or which contain colonialist or otherwise disagreeable themes. While that might not be good per se, they haven't transformed global culture to become more violent.

Instead, we can definitively say that gamer *culture*, as a subset of online culture, radicalizes young men to the right-wing. The reason is that the *communities* surrounding video gaming have become a cesspool of right-wing political activity and thought throughout the world. It's not the games that are the problem, but the kinds of communities people have made around them. This is what Linda Schlegel, Rachel Kowert, and their co-authors argue in *Gaming and Extremism*, a recent book that analyzes how and why video games became a vector of radicalization for young men. Many video games offer online social spaces in the game itself via text or voice chatting, in addition to the active online communities they spin off on other platforms. It's largely the content of these communities, rather than the content of the games themselves, that carries the potential for extremist radicalization.

The culture surrounding video games has long been a source of unsettling messages that are sexist and racist.[3] But things have escalated in the last decade, with video game culture being directly tied to real-life political positions. This is no more apparent than in the case of GamerGate.

GamerGate was a primarily online social movement focused on harassing female video game producers, voice actors, players, as well as the companies they worked for or bought from. Its name comes from the movement itself, which purported to be a way of exposing how video game culture was becoming infected by malicious, outside forces trying to take something good from the people—if that sounds familiar after Chapter 1's discussions of the origins of fascist logic, that's because it should.

GamerGate began with attacks on video game designer Zoe Quinn, a nonbinary game developer who produced a game called Depression Quest. After its release, a former partner of Quinn's posted a scathing, abusive blog about their relationship, alleging that Quinn received a positive review of their game in exchange for a sexual relationship with its reviewer. This relationship never occurred, and indeed the reviewer involved in the conspiracy theory never reviewed any of Quinn's content, but this didn't matter to the online mob. Quinn—a nonbinary, assigned female at birth game developer—was targeted because they were producing video games that bucked the trends dominant among those who considered themselves to be the "true gamers," that is, young men who mostly played violent and competitive online games, congregating on websites like 4chan, 8chan, and Reddit. This mob produced a campaign of violent harassment against Quinn and their family, including thousands of death threats and hacking many of their personal accounts.

Another target of the GamerGate mob was Anita Sarkeesian, a woman who has made a career of taking video games seriously as an artistic medium. Her commentary typically focuses on the gendered and sexual aspects of video games, both aesthetically and structurally, and she became famous initially for discussing gender and gender politics in video games. Sarkeesian also received death threats, threats to sexually assault her, threats to attack her and her family, and numerous attempts and successes in hacking into her personal accounts. The severity of this threat roused the attention of the FBI, which takes open calls to mass violence seriously. Sarkeesian was also targeted for her ethnicity. Many online harassers assumed, based on her appearance, that she is Jewish. This resulted in a torrent of anti-Semitic harassment, unaffected by the fact that Sarkeesian is ethnically Armenian.

GamerGate is an important example of far-right content and online culture because it exemplifies many of its most important features. It was a coordinated, organized campaign, but it didn't have an overarching leadership or central organization. Instead, it came from dozens of diffuse sources, message boards, and chat groups all at once. There were central figures, but they were themselves largely anonymous as they harassed their victims. This made identifying perpetrators or stopping the harassment difficult.

GamerGate is also a good example of how right-wing messaging can hide in other kinds of political or social commentary. On the surface, the public messages put out by various GamerGate conspiracy theorists were about video game journalism and design, as well as the culture of video game players. GamerGate participants argued that gaming *was* simply a predominantly male space, and that trying to change that was an affront to the men who played games. They also argued that games like Quinn's Depression Quest didn't deserve to be included alongside what they considered to be "real games," those that featured violence and conflict. Of course, these arguments were just screens for the fact that GamerGate was a coordinated harassment campaign against women involved in a male-dominated industry—it was an earnest effort to preserve the patriarchal nature of video game culture.

The GamerGate campaign itself lost steam around 2016, but its effect on online culture can still be felt—in 2024, its current manifestation is the obsession with "woke" culture in games and media. Countless commentators take to dozens of platforms to trash media franchises from Marvel movies to the Lord of the Rings to, bizarrely, Star Trek for what they consider to be their recent turn to social liberalism, by which they mean gender and racial representation. Many of these fans consider themselves to be protecting the purity or canon of the works they are fans of, thinking that corporate and social movement interests are united in efforts to ruin these media.

Of course, these conspiracies do not exist, but imagining them has fed countless young men into right-wing circles. This can be proven anecdotally and sociologically. We know from personal testimony that David DePape, who invaded the home of then US Speaker of the House Nancy Pelosi and attacked her husband with a hammer, claimed he was directly inspired and radicalized toward the right-wing by GamerGate.[4] We also know that discussions about GamerGate directed people to conservative and right-wing sources on other media platforms and that they originated in and were primarily circulated on some of the most right-wing spaces online. Beyond these individual perpetrators, researchers agree that GamerGate helped create the social media landscape that would eventually produce the Groypers and other large online communities that foster extremism.

In the aftermath of GamerGate, video game culture has become a common way for the right-wing to wind its way into the lives and media consumption of young men. This happens both in the games themselves and in the form of video game influencers.

Many online games today allow, or even require, direct player-to-player conversation and interaction. As intended, these conversations would allow players to coordinate their strategies, participate in role-playing, or simply socialize. Studies of these conversations show that these interactions often involve a vastly disproportionate amount of anti-LGBTQ, sexist, and racial slurs, even when compared to the conversations of otherwise extremely bigoted people.[5] While sometimes dismissed as playground banter, the kind of thing that all children and teens go through as they test boundaries, these conversations and their bigoted language serve to construct a culture that assumes that white men, and in this case only young white men, are present and deserving of respect. Other identities are seen as deserving of ridicule and exclusion if they can't handle this kind of verbal violence.

For many young men, these spaces might be the first place they hear certain slurs, especially if their families are leftist or liberal. It might be the first time they hear people their age laugh at a racist, sexist, or ableist joke. This can cause young men to latch onto these behaviors and defend them against critics even when they know the harm they do. This means that video games are a common space for the right-wing radicalization of young men.

However, don't hastily decide that the answer is banning your son from playing them! That option is one that might cause your son to resent you, especially if he knows why you've made that decision. Banning games in order to protect him from an ideology you disagree with might be the best way to make him more curious about that ideology. This is why you need to *talk to your son* about the things he might hear in those forums before he hears them.

If you want to talk to your son about video game culture, start with questions that show earnest curiosity about his life and his online relationships. Avoid starting the conversation with accusations or with any leading statements about how video games are dangerous or always associated with violence or extremism. Treat this as an opportunity to get to know your son and his hobbies!

Here are some possible avenues for you to start your conversation:

* What kinds of games are you playing now? What's your favorite? What do you like about it?
* Do you play that alone, or with friends?
* Did you know those friends from regular life, or did you meet them online?
* What do you like to talk to them about? What do you like about them as friends?

After you've gotten off on the right foot, continue by asking them about these online friends just like you would ask about any of their friends. Ask what they talk about together and seek out examples of interactions between them that show what kinds of jokes they laugh about or stories they tell. Use this information to inform what you need to pay attention to in the future. It might turn out that your son's online friendships are stable and healthy and that they aren't leading him to something right-wing. If you do hear worrying signs—like racist, sexist, or homophobic language, for example—then keep this in mind as you move on to the conversation strategies listed in Chapter 4.

Influencers

Many young people, young men included, get a lot of their entertainment and perspective from online "influencers," people who make content on the internet, and particularly on platforms like YouTube, Instagram, or TikTok. These people can sometimes pass themselves off as experts in what they do, whether that's fashion, fitness, cooking, etc. Others are essentially only celebrities, famous because of their fame or their looks.

One of the most famous and successful content producers in the world is a perfect example of this. Felix Kjellberg, better known by his online name PewDiePie, started producing video game content on YouTube in 2010. By the mid-2010s, his channel was the most subscribed on the platform, producing a massive amount of content that expanded from mostly consisting of video game playthroughs to including small skits and expanded long-form jokes. He's since faded from the limelight, but his story is a good example of how apparently innocent influencers intersect with right-wing content.

It was his humor that got Kjellberg connected with the right-wing. Like many young men of his generation, Kjellberg has a disruptive and transgressive sense of humor. He's made jokes about rape and sexual assault, jokes about fascism and Nazis, and jokes about white supremacy that he assures his viewers and media outlets are done just for fun. He's used the n-word live while streaming to millions and is known to have followed openly white supremacist accounts.[6] This has made him a perfect way for a young person to get connected with right-wing content online. A young man might follow Kjellberg because of his video game content, laugh at some of his jokes, hear that the media and others disapprove of his humor, and then start to feel a sense of connection with the online communities that support him rather than with his critics.

Disconnecting from the mainstream and finding a home online, racist content is precisely what happens to many young men as they move to the right. Though Kjellberg has largely retired from being an online celebrity, his style has influenced numerous other streamers who use comedic video game content as a Trojan Horse for fascism. His media personality has also made its way directly into right-wing violence—as Brandon Tarrant began his massacre at the Christchurch Mosque in New Zealand, he suggested to anyone watching his live stream to "subscribe to PewDiePie."[7]

Other influencers offer explicitly political content. Often, this content is in the shape of media criticism or lifestyle advice, rather than discussing policy or politics openly. Many right-wing influencers, for example, on YouTube, present their content as media criticism. Along with some media analysis of a movie, for example, they might decry its "woke agenda"—by which they might mean anything from the movie's inclusion of a homosexual character to racially blind casting. This narrative is often presented as a "fall from grace" story, one about the left, progressives, or sometimes very openly simply women in general gaining control over a property. There's been an explosion of this type of critique of Marvel and Star Wars properties, for example, regarding the inclusion of female protagonists, and of Amazon's Lord of the Rings series for its casting of a Black woman as a Dwarf.

These critiques have nothing to do with the artistic or entertainment merit of these properties—they're about the political and social context that they're operating in. Commentators who complain about this kind of inclusiveness are upset because other people are prioritizing real-world political issues such as gender, racial, and sexual inclusion over integrity to the original design of media properties that were created by white men. Sometimes, they critique the "woke" agenda of media properties that have always had radically progressive agendas, such as Star Trek.

Enumerating these influencers and their channels would be an exercise in futility—there are simply too many of them, and more and more crop up every day. Most are small, with few followers, but some make their living off producing this kind of content, regularly releasing videos proclaiming that "woke culture" has ruined their culture. These creators are using their platforms to spread racist and sexist ideas. Their goal is to argue against the existence of male privilege and white privilege, claiming that when the media becomes more diverse, it also becomes worse.

For many young men and young people in general, these videos might be the first time they see any kind of media criticism at all. It might be the first time that they feel like someone is talking to them without talking down to them, like a teacher or parent would. Instead, this content approaches the listener and viewer as a fellow fan or gamer—as an equal. And instead of talking about a novel they've been assigned in school, they're discussing something the viewer cares about, like a game, show, or movie. These videos allow them to see themselves as part of a community of like-minded people who care about something enough to want to protect it.

That feeling, in and of itself, is a good one—it helps people think of their world and their opinions about it as something worthy of sharing with others. Young people forming communities and developing friendships online is a good thing, and something you should encourage just as you'd encourage your son to make friends anywhere else. The issue isn't with finding community online, or in video games, or in being a fan of an online celebrity. It's with what some of those communities lead young people to.

The other problem is that most of the time, these videos and their perspectives don't challenge anyone's ideas. Algorithms work by showing people what they think the user *will* like, not by showing them things they think they might disagree with. This powerful confirmation bias reinforces itself, something you're probably familiar with if you're a user of a service like YouTube, Instagram, or TikTok. If you watch a form of content, the service will show you more of it—that's how they make their money, by learning your preferences, selling that information to third parties, and using those preferences to sell ads.

When it comes to political preferences, though, this means that most social media platforms and content-sharing apps end up being enormous echo chambers. Users who start to encounter right-wing content and watch some of it, either out of some initial interest or simply curiosity, will end up seeing more of that same kind of content.

There are several other kinds of online influencers that act as gateways to increasingly radical right-wing content. Some influencers, for example, are essentially professional misogynists. They make their money and achieve their fame by denigrating women, promoting views and behaviors that seek to reduce the place and power of women in society, and even openly advocate for sexual violence and rape.

The influence of men who promote rape culture is nothing new in the United States or the rest of the world—examples from movies, books, songs, and other media throughout the 20th century are too many to count. Men who have short-term sexual relationships with multiple women—for example, characters like James

Bond—have been popular among young men for decades, while men's media and magazines promise secrets for how to seduce women and convince them to have sex with you.

Today, though, there's a difference—influencers openly talk about their "conquests" in a direct, personal way, emulating the kinds of conversations men have in private about their sexual and romantic lives. Presenting their "exploits" in this light makes them seem more relatable and approachable and puts their comments in a context that will be more palatable for the young men who consume their content.

That content, though, is often disturbing and sexually violent. Some of these influencers are part of an online subculture called "PUA," or pick-up artists, and their content is almost exclusively advice about how to trick, cajole, or pressure women into having sex with men. In addition to promoting sexual gratification, this content promotes the perspective that women exist to be manipulated by men into having sex with them. Often, these men talk about women as something to be conquered and counted—another number in the list of people they've had sex with.

This in and of itself is objectionable and something you should steer your son clear of. It's sexist, exploitative, and in some cases literally promotes sexual assault or rape. Beyond the harm that this causes to the individual women who are targeted by these men, though, the PUA movement has had a profound effect on the right-wing at large. Since the 2000s, this subculture has been directly connected to the growth of the right-wing. PUA leaders and promoters, such as Roosh V, Mike Cernovich, and others, have linked their predatory pursuit of sex with a dedication to right-wing causes.[8] Roosh V, born Daryush Valizadeh, ran the blog "Return of Kings," which advocated for men to take power in their communities and relationships and suggested to young white men in Western countries that they could go to the Global South and control women more easily there. He has since turned right-wing Christian and repudiated his advocacy for casual sex. Mike Cernovich is another anti-feminist blogger who advocated for masculine power and privilege, was deeply involved in GamerGate, and also the Trump campaign in 2016, though he has since tried to distance himself from these communities.

A more recent and obvious connector between "pick-up artists" and the right-wing is the case of Andrew Tate. Tate was a professional kickboxer and a contestant on a British reality show in 2016 but was fired from the show due to his misogynist and otherwise bigoted comments. He rode the controversy of his statements to stardom, however, by offering classes and other paid content online.

Tate's money came from a series of online pyramid schemes, selling get-rich-quick opportunities that preyed on those who looked up to him for how much money he had and how successful he was at getting people to pay him for looking rich. One such scheme, "Hustler's University," saw participants paying him to get advice about how to make money, primarily from non-traditional means online. They would also be compensated for bringing more people into the platform, resulting in enough attention to it as a pyramid scheme that the hosts of the website shut it down. Tate has since rebranded and relaunched this platform.

Tate built a brand as the kind of man that a teenage boy might aspire to be. He's physically strong and ostentatiously rich. He's got dozens of fancy cars and big expensive houses to live in. His videos frequently feature him showing off his homes, cars, and other expensive things like suits, food, and gadgets. This does little to differentiate him from other "lifestyle influencers," people who make their living off their appearances on the internet by accumulating social media platform followers and getting advertisers to pay them to feature their products. If this were all Tate was, he'd be a tasteless influence and little more.

But Tate's brand has another, much more sinister side in addition to him showing off his wealth or preying on those who are financially unstable. Tate dedicates much of his content, including many of his classes, to offering tips and advice to young men on how to deal with women, especially women they want to pursue romantically or sexually. A vital part of his brand as a powerful male influencer is his claim to have dozens of girlfriends at a time, all of them young and conventionally beautiful. He frequently has them appear in his videos and other messaging, in a curious combination of bragging to his audience and claiming to be able to tell them how they can get in his position.

Tate both implicitly and explicitly subscribes to the stereotypical assumptions about gender and sexual roles. He assumes that his viewers are male and that they're heterosexual. He assumes that their goal is to have penetrative sex with as many women as possible and claims to be a success story in this regard, sometimes offering up his "number" by means of bragging and selling the advice he has to offer. His advice is straightforward and cuts through most normative gender assumptions. Whereas most traditional gender roles present women as something complicated that men have to try to understand, like some kind of puzzle that needs to be unlocked, Tate and those like him tell young men that women are, in fact, very simple. For Tate, women are simple machines that evaluate whether it's worth it for them to sleep with someone. If you are rich and powerful enough and if you're physically strong enough, they will desire you—whether they know it or not.

This depiction of what women want does not originate with Tate, and it won't stop with him either. It's a common trope in the online spaces where Tate thrived, particularly in misogynist circles on social media platforms. Having claimed to have "solved" women, Tate then goes on to sell his methods for becoming financially and physically successful in order to be desirable. After all, his claim is that if you simply become desirable enough, women will naturally want to be with you.

Another important claim of Tate's, and most other influencers in the same spaces, is that women actually *like* being treated with disrespect and distaste. He tells young men that women want to be seen as only sex objects, and that they all want to be associated with whatever is the most successful man they can viably attach themselves to. This is the core of the "pickup artist" method for attracting women. The idea is that men can use simple social tools to manipulate women into wanting to sleep with them, without the women knowing that they're being manipulated in this way. Most of these methods consist of advising men to act in cocky and cruel ways not just to women but to other men around them, insulting people with varying degrees of subtlety, acting entitled to other people's time and bodies, and immediately taking charge of any situation they find themselves in.

But Tate is also clear that these methods won't work for everyone—and this is a vital aspect of his appeal. His message isn't that any man can get beautiful women to flock to him, but instead that only the most successful men will get any women to be interested in them at all. This complicates the typical self-help narrative that promises a quick fix. Instead, Tate shows pity for most of his audience and tells them that it might be too little, too late for them when it comes to being a desirable man. Some of them, he says, might simply be too short, too unattractive, or too feminine to get women at all. The insulting nature of this content might seem to make its popularity confusing, but Tate always expresses what seems to be real pity for the men watching his content who feel they fall into this category. Some of his most popular videos consist of him talking with the beautiful women he surrounds himself with and telling them that they'll never understand the struggles of the young men he's talking to because they will never have to face the same kind of rejection. He claims that women will never understand the struggles of young men who aren't typically socially desirable because of their appearance or their wealth.

This appeal to sympathy and understanding is the second part of Tate's message, and it's also key to the way that other influencers try to get young men on their side. Combining pity for young cis men with disdain for women lets Tate and those like him occupy a curious position that combines earnestness with anger and resentment.

Tate himself has been canceled in every possible sense of the word for some time now. He's been banned from most social media platforms and many funding sources and has had his websites removed by their hosts. More importantly, he's also been arrested for human trafficking in Romania, where he and his brother moved after explicitly commenting that they went there in order to take advantage of the country's relatively lax sexual assault legislation.

While Tate himself remains popular even after his arrests, that's not really the point. The issue isn't his personal popularity but instead the fact that people like Tate are massively successful and influential. Their content provides an avenue of radicalization for young men who are simply consuming the kind of content that one might assume they would—comedy aimed at teenagers and young men in their 20s. Online communities that produce and share such content, along with platforms that algorithmically suggest content they believe the viewer might want to see, work to move users to the extremes of their viewpoints by encouraging them out of their comfort zones.

Tate himself is unlikely to come back to the level of popularity and influence he enjoyed before his arrest. His recent appearances online have been mocked by many who once unironically looked up to him or even considered him godlike. But

Fitness Influence Content ⇨ Dating Advice ⇨ Male Supremacism ⇨ Fascism

Video Game Content ⇨ Jokes about "Girl Gamers" ⇨ GamerGate ⇨ Fascism

Edgy, Clickbait Videos or TikToks ⇨ Conspiracy Theory Content ⇨ Anti-Semitic Content ⇨ Fascism

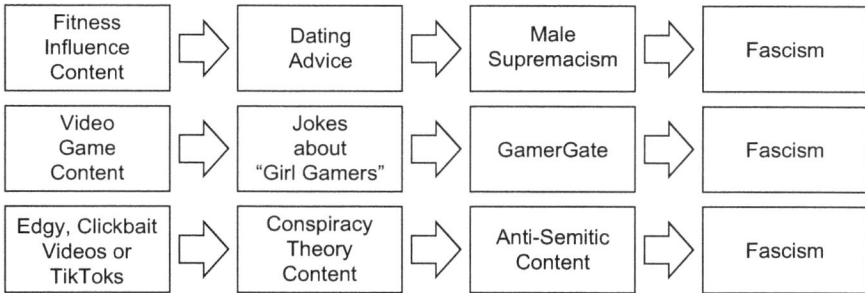

FIGURE 3.1   This chart shows how online content that you might not bat an eye at can lead to increasingly worrying content. This isn't an exhaustive list.

Source: Author's creation.

while his own brand and time in the sun might be gone, tarnished for his followers less because of his arrest for human trafficking than for his bizarre social media posts after he emerged from jail, he's brought to the popular consciousness a form of cartoonish masculine posing that proved to be incredibly successful and appealing to millions of young men all over the world.

FIGURE 3.1 is a flowchart that shows how content that seems innocuous can potentially lead to increasingly right-wing content online. On the left is content your son might encounter innocently or which you might not have any concern about. This then leads to less palatable subjects, like dating advice, sexist jokes, or conspiracy theories, which can then lead further to openly right-wing content.

This isn't meant to be an exhaustive or comprehensive list of ways that your son might reach right-wing content online. Instead, I've included it to help you see how memes, jokes, and other content that you might not blink an eye at can lead down surprising paths to openly extreme right-wing influences.

How Social Media Spreads Hate

I spoke with Callum Hood, the head of research at the Center for Countering Digital Hate (which, as I write this, is being threatened with a lawsuit from Elon Musk for its investigations into how his social media company enables the spread of extremist politics). The CCDH conducts research in the English-speaking world on the connections between online extremist content and extremist beliefs. "What we focus on is how social media platforms spread hate," says Hood. "For most types of hate, there is sophisticated machinery that spreads from the extremists to the mainstream, even if the connections between those two can be unclear or complicated. There's efforts by the extremists to make their content more palatable to the mainstream or traditional media, so that it's picked up by a wider audience."

One example of this process, Hood says, comes in the form of anti-queer messaging. "When I first started working at CCDH, I remember seeing some very extreme accounts on Instagram posting vicious stuff about trans people, likening LGBTQ people, calls to treat them with respect, or even their very existence as a push for some sort of sinister ideology—one that harms and sexualizes children. At the time, this was limited to those accounts. Now, years later, this perspective gets huge traction on mainstream social media platforms; it's contributed to the popularization of the term 'groomer.'" Here, Hood is referring to a common right-wing insult for queer people and their allies, 'groomer,' which implies that their goal is to get more young people to be queer or trans—part of a centuries-old claim that homosexuals and other sexually or gender nonconforming people are pedophiles.

Hood at the CCDH says that people can help their efforts to reduce the spread of extremism online by pressuring elected officials. "We're calling for online hate to be a more electoral issue. We live so much of our lives online, and what happens online has real effects on our lives; it can have effects on democracy, and it can make it harder to live as a minority—these are all electoral issues!"

The CCDH is part of a growing movement to have protections against the spread of extremist rhetoric online made into law. "We want to demand transparency from these companies and put basic public safety standards in place for how platforms are accessed and used by their youngest users. We need people to talk to their elected officials about this—ask them questions about what they're doing to regulate the spread of hate on social media."

Hood emphasizes that this doesn't mean an end to free speech online. "We can do this in a way that's completely consistent with maintaining the things we like about social media: that everyone can access it, that everyone can express themselves freely on it. We just need to demand that we make an internet that has the positives of online life without the huge advantage it currently delivers to hate and disinformation."

There are legal and electoral campaigns in many countries pushing for this kind of legislation. Right-wing content creators, of course, are constantly pushing against these moves. They argue that any changes that make it harder to access their content are an attack against freedom of speech or possibly the result of a vast international conspiracy to suppress their worldview. This perspective is unfortunately shared by some of the most powerful people in social media, including Elon Musk. His recent purchase of Twitter, now X, has resulted in a cascade of changes to how the platform is moderated. Since his seizure of the company, it has jettisoned most of its content moderators, especially those who focus on disinformation and hate speech, all supposedly in the name of Musk's "free speech absolutism."

Of course, when free speech comes for the right-wing, they complain and demand protection. The online right-wing thinks of itself as a perpetual victim, always being persecuted. For example, when social media accounts call out racist language or campaign against misinformation, right-wing sources push back against them and claim that they've been targeted unfairly.

In other words, the right-wing understands that online platforms are battlefields for the hearts and minds of everyday people. They use social media, intentionally, to produce propaganda.

We know for a fact that the creators of much right-wing online content are very aware that they're producing propaganda. Their forums and chats discuss this explicitly, not just bragging about how they are moving people to the right but offering suggestions for their fellow content creators about how to do so more effectively.

One such creator is Andrew Anglin, a neo-Nazi writer and the runner of the largest openly fascist web community in the United States, the "Daily Stormer." Named after the Nazi Party newspaper *Der Stürmer*, the Daily Stormer is a message board and content-sharing website that intentionally produces fascist and right-wing content with the goal of reaching people who aren't already right-wing. Anglin and those who use the website push themselves to make memes, videos, and other content that packages right-wing ideology in jokes, cultural references, and everyday internet content to make it more palatable to people who wouldn't seek out white supremacist or anti-Semitic content on their own.

Anglin has gone so far as to write a guide for radicalizing people, called *Redpilling Normies*. Both of these words are right-wing memes. "Redpilling" comes from the first "Matrix" movie, in which the main character, living in a computer-generated world, is offered a choice between a blue pill that will keep him in his delusion and a red one that will wake him up to the real world. This metaphor is deep in the right-wing imagination and is often used when talking about "opening someone's eyes" to the way the world really works. Anglin and his allies use what might look like jokes to push radicalizing content into more and more mainstream spaces.

Oliver Goodman works at Moonshot, a tech company that works with social media platforms to try to show people off-ramps to radicalizing online content. Generally speaking, he says, people don't go to the internet seeking radical content with no prompting. Instead, they come to it gradually, through communities that aren't themselves explicitly designed for the dissemination of extremist messages. They come to these groups seeking "fraternity, a group of like-minded individuals," and leave with a sense that they might have found a group of people they could belong to. It's only after the community has become an inviting home that its right-wing content starts to become increasingly obvious.

Andrew Pel, Head of Campaigns at Moonshot, described Moonshot's method as one of "de-escalation" and "disengagement" rather than "de-radicalization." Describing the process in the abstract, he asked me to "imagine someone—a young man—who's searching online for incel content. Maybe he's watching a YouTube video about the social isolation he's experiencing, which is what's motivating his connection to the idea of being an incel." From Chapter 2, you already know what could happen to such a young man. He might find himself falling down a rabbit hole of increasingly sexist incel content. And as if that weren't already bad enough and capable of leading him to commit verbal and physical violence, that could lead to him gaining an interest in the Groypers or other openly white supremacist groups that also express sexist views and argue that men deserve sex and companionship from women.

The goal is to provide an alternative to this content. "What we do is that when this guy is searching for this content, we also show him other ads about social isolation, except that these ones are for connecting him to real mental health and social work practices. By showing these ads alongside the incel content, we've facilitated an interaction with service providers," says Pel. After that, it's up to the user, the person who searched for this content, to click on their messaging and hopefully follow it to some form of social service or mental health provision.

So, while there are a lot of right-wingers online who are trying to radicalize your son and other young men, there are also people out in the world trying to stop that from happening.[9] And if you're looking for resources and strategies that you can use for yourself if you're worried about your son being radicalized online, there are guides and suggestions at the end of this chapter.

In-person Radicalization

Despite all the fear-mongering and attention given to online radicalization, it's important to remember that right-wing radicalization can happen in person as well. It can come from your son's fellow young people at school, church, or other communities, or it can come from adults such as relatives and mentors.

Like most political beliefs that are outside the mainstream, fascism develops and recruits heavily on college campuses. While left-wing radicalization is more often associated with college attendance, right-wing groups also target college students for recruitment.

Of course, the groups that target college students for radicalization are generally different from those that might seek out non-college-attending members. These groups are often less crass and less openly militant than the paramilitary organizations that operate off-campus, such as the Atomwaffen, Patriot Front, or the Traditionalist Workers' Party. Instead, right-wing organizations on college campuses generally present themselves as more palatable and professional than their counterparts.

One clear example of right-wing radicalization on a college campus can be found at the University of California, Berkeley, a college famous for its history of left-wing organizing and radicalization in the 1960s and 70s. However, it might surprise you to learn that the largest student organization on the Berkeley campus is the College Republicans!

The College Republicans are a national organization affiliated with the Republican Party but generally not organized parts of the party itself. Instead, they're independent groups of young people who support the GOP agenda and seek to develop young Republican leaders. They also serve as an important pipeline to volunteering and employment in the Republican Party and for work in other conservative

organizations. These groups have produced several key GOP leaders, from gover-
nors and senators to policy advocates and advisors.

Many College Republican chapters are innocuous, mainstream conservative
organizations that conduct get-out-the-vote campaigns on and surrounding their
campuses, engage in fundraising, and stage political conversations. Others, though,
have a much more radical bent. The Berkeley College Republicans are one such
group, having developed a significant right-wing bent. This has led them to invite
speakers who aren't just members of the GOP mainstream but who are instead on
its right-wing fringes, such as Milo Yiannopoulos and Ann Coulter.

A more openly right-wing campus organization in the United States is Turning
Point USA. Founded by young activist Charlie Kirk with money from a conservative businessman, TP USA seeks to organize on college campuses and redirect
young people toward right-wing politics. Kirk himself dropped out of college in
order to pursue this goal and, as of this publication, has never gotten a college
education.

The stated goal of TP USA is to "combat liberalism on college and university
campuses," and it does so through political activism, organizing debates and events,
and running a series of scaremongering events aimed at inspiring fear in leftists on
campus.[10] One of its initiatives, the Professor Watchlist, is a website that features
profiles and write-ups of professors that TP USA and its student members accuse of
being leftists or of promoting leftism on campus, supposedly based on reviews and
tips left by students at those campuses. TP USA claims that these professors violate
the standards of objectivity necessary for college settings.

But this is only the tip of the iceberg when it comes to TP USA's activities—its
goal is to be the leading conservative and right-wing organization among young
people, specifically young college-educated, in the United States. To achieve this
goal, TP USA funnels money into other campus organizations, trying to help these
conservative and right-wing forces take over their respective college governments
and put on events that will change the atmosphere of the campus to such a degree
that those who aren't right-wing feel less comfortable.

Of course, the most likely place a young person will encounter fascist perspectives is at home. Nick Fuentes, the most influential young fascist in the United
States, happily cites his parents as the source of his right-wing thinking and even
has his parents as guests on his show at times. As I said in the intro, I assume that
if you've bought and are reading this book, you're not a fascist and aren't going to
radicalize your own son, but that doesn't mean you don't have to be careful about
what you say and do around him.

Fascist radicalization doesn't look like it might in a movie, with someone getting handed a flier to attend a rally and finding themselves swept up in it. Instead,
we have to pay attention to what led up to their seeing these messages and being
interested in them at all. That means looking at their home and community.

Even if you're not a fascist, you've got to be careful about how you talk and act
around your son to make sure that your behavior doesn't ease into an approach to

fascism. Jokes that focus on racial or gender stereotypes can teach a young man that it's ok, or even funny, to discriminate against people based on the color of their skin, the religion they practice, or where they're from. Anti-Semitic jokes and attitudes are especially important to guard against in this respect, as this form of racial discrimination is probably the most associated with fascism.

Other means of right-wing radicalization are more direct still. It's unlikely that an adult will turn to your son and directly ask him if he's interested in joining a far-right-wing organization. In fact, it's important to remember that most people on the far right, just like the far left, aren't actively members of anything and don't go out marching or protesting. Most people live their lives without actively recruiting people to their perspective.

Instead, the most likely thing that might happen is your son hearing a sexist or racist joke from an elderly relative, or hearing them say something bigoted. In these contexts, it's important to always respond to that bigoted statement to be sure that your son—and any other young people around—know that those sentiments can't go unanswered. It's not enough to tell your son that these people are from a different time and that they might just be telling those "jokes" or saying those things because they don't know any better. All that does is teach your son that there are some people who are allowed to say these taboo things and get away with it, and that there are some people who believe them earnestly and don't get questioned for it. Especially if your son has started saying those jokes himself, you don't have the luxury of telling him to ignore these things.

What Right-Wing Activity Looks Like

With the exception of Trump's attempted coup in 2021, most of the right-wing activity happening in the United States today comes from decentralized communities. This kind of organization promotes a level of disconnection that means that when its members engage in violence, its leaders can claim to not have been responsible—after all, they aren't really the *leaders* of anything since nobody elected them, and they have no power other than the power that comes from people choosing to listen to them.

Communities like this are where the term "Lone Wolf" comes from. Popularized in the 1990s, the mythos surrounding the Lone Wolf has infected the ways that people talk about right-wing political violence, especially violence committed by people who aren't openly part of some paramilitary organization or card-carrying members of an extremist group. Lone wolves are usually young, though some are middle-aged. This supposed separation from formal right-wing political involvement is what differentiates them from the kinds of extremist violence we see in the 20th century, with pitched street battles between right-wing forces and those on the left.

These militants and their supposed isolation have become central to the way that people think about far-right violence. Their independence has become a badge of honor for many of the young people who aspire to be like them—they're alone, fighting the good fight, doing what needs to be done to defend their culture and community, even at the risk of losing their place in that community or their very lives. This appearance of selflessness is part of the mystique and appeal of the "lone wolf," and it's something that even non-right-wing media leans into when discussing them and their behavior. These militants are treated as if they come from nowhere—parents and friends are interviewed to see if they had shown any warning signs before their violent outbursts or if they were surprised by them.

This individualizing perspective on their violence also allows commentators to present it as a symptom of mental illness or generalized social decay, rather than as a form of political commitment. In the wake of the Columbine school shootings in Colorado, the media grasped at dozens of possible interpretations of those young men's violence, from what video games they played to what psychiatric medicine or care they were consuming.

Framing their violence as a form of mental illness completely removes it from any political or intentional context that the perpetrator might have intended or imagined for his violence. This not only strips these young men of their agency—an agency they used to commit acts of horrible violence—but it pathologizes their politics rather than taking it seriously as an opposing viewpoint. Treating their motives as the result of mental health problems rather than actual political or social commitment lets us hold it at arm's length. Instead of trying to understand it, we can just avoid it and brush it under the rug, calling it the result of too many violent video games or of social isolation when we should be confronting it as a different belief system, a different way of thinking about the world. A monstrous way of thinking about it, a terrible one, yes, but still a coherent belief system that needs to be met head-on.

Lone wolves simply aren't alone. Their ideology and practice don't come from nowhere. These men are not sitting at home, coming to the same conclusions about how to target people, how to build pipe bombs, or where to get the best guns for mass shootings. They're talking to fellow white supremacists and sexists; they're in touch with older generations of neo-Nazis; they're reading guides posted online about how to arm themselves and how to engage in mass violence.

In fact, the term "lone wolf" comes from the very right-wing communities these lone wolves are supposedly not connected to—it's not a term used by academics or those who pay attention to the right-wing except when we're talking to the public. Starting in the 1980s, right-wing sources started to call for "lone wolves" to take matters into their own hands and commit acts of violence on their behalf precisely because they were too weak and disorganized to mount a group effort—and because they thought that having individuals commit these acts, rather than groups as with the KKK's violence in the 1960s and 70s, would hide them from view.

And they were right—rather than thinking about "lone wolf" violence as the way that disorganized right-wing movements coordinate their attacks, without elected leaders and bureaucracies but still featuring group effort and planning, common sense encourages people to see these acts of violence as random, individual, or more recently "stochastic." All of these terms imply that this violence is simply random and unconnected to ideological commitments.

We know, though, that the vast majority of people who have been called "lone wolves" did in fact have an ideology. They left behind manifestos, online presences, and other signs that clearly point to their political bent. And the overwhelming majority of political violence done in the last several decades has been committed by the extreme right—and that's not just in the United States and Europe.

This is the ultimate problem of the Lone Wolf framing—it allows the media and popular consciousness to play directly into the hands of the right-wing promoters of that perspective, making this violence seem individual and even random when it is in fact anything but. Lone wolves may commit their violence alone, but they do so after months or years of participating in forums and communities that are dedicated to the promotion of right-wing ideologies. Their ideas, their targets, and their tactics come from other people in these communities—in fact, often from leaders and influencers who have dedicated their lives to nurturing hatred and violence in others. Lone wolves act alone, but they don't come from nowhere.

Ultimately, the lone wolf concept is a way to talk about terrorist acts committed by white men without using the same language that most mainstream media uses when discussing attacks committed by people of color, and especially Muslims. Many attacks that are falsely attributed to Islam in the mainstream press are committed by individuals acting alone on the day of the attack, and some of them are committed by people who are apparently disconnected from larger terrorist organizations. Yet the term "lone wolf" conjures up images of a white man with a gun.

Making a list of right-wing influencers, websites, and apps is very difficult—it'll be outdated the day after you make it due to how quickly the sands shift in online communities. But if you want a list of people to keep an eye and ear out for, or a list of apps to wonder if your son is on, here's one. Remember, this is just a starting point! Ask your son what personalities, apps, and message boards he's on, and then look them up or check them out yourself.

List of US-focused Right-Wing Commentators and Sources:

- Andrew Tate
  - Former MMA fighter, influencer, and human trafficker, known for misogyny
- Jordan Peterson
  - Former psychology professor at the University of Toronto, now right-wing self-help guru and media personality

- Nick Fuentes
  - Host of the America First show, a streaming talk show full of extreme right-wing content, also famous for dining at Mar-a-Lago with former President Trump and right-wing rapper Ye (formerly Kanye West)
- Hannah Pearl Davis (JustPearlyThings)
  - Misogynist and anti-feminist influencer, promoter of so-called traditional or "trad" feminine roles
- Alex Jones
  - Right-wing conspiracy theorist and talk show host, most famous for claiming that the Sandy Hook massacre was faked (this has since lost him a lawsuit with the parents of the children who were killed in that attack)
- Ben Shapiro
  - Host of several right-wing talk media platforms, including podcasts and video streams, former editor at Breitbart News, author, and general right-wing provocateur
- Tim Pool
  - Part of a team of right-wing influencers and video promoters called Tenet Media, Pool has long been a major feature of online right-wing commentary. As I write this in the fall of 2024, Pool and his associates are under scrutiny for possibly being Russian misinformation puppets.
- Laura Loomer
  - Loomer is an open white nationalist who ran in 2020 to represent Florida's 21st Congressional district but lost. She remains a powerful right-wing influencer, advocating a mix of conspiracy theories and fascist rhetoric.
- Steve Bannon
  - Steven Bannon was Donald Trump's central campaign advisor in the 2016 election and is often cited as the reason for Trump's victory. Bannon is a true believer in the right-wing claim that Western civilization is on the decline. As I write this in the fall of 2024, he's currently in prison for failing to comply with a US Congressional subpoena

Here's a list of right-wing and conservative apps and websites:

- 4chan, 8chan/8kun
  - These websites originated as anime fan message boards but have since become the origin of much right-wing social media messaging and memes.

4chan presents itself as playful and non-serious while sharing racist, sexist, and otherwise right-wing content. 8chan (now 8kun) is more openly right-wing and is specifically the origin of the QAnon conspiracy theory.

- KiwiFarms

  - KiwiFarms is an online harassment website dedicated to identifying and persecuting people online and in real life. Users find vulnerable people and celebrities and coordinate intense cyberbullying and other harassing campaigns in an attempt to ruin their lives or encourage them to commit suicide. In some cases, they have succeeded. I *strongly* recommend avoiding this website.

- Gab

  - Gab is a social media platform designed as a "free speech" space that caters to the extreme right-wing, particularly those who have been banned or pushed out of other platforms.

- TRUTH Social

  - This is the social media company that Donald Trump funded after his loss in the 2020 presidential election and his ban from Twitter following his attempted coup.

- BitChute

  - BitChute is an alternative to YouTube, much like Gab or TRUTH Social for video-format content.

- Telegram

  - Founded by Pavel Durov, Telegram is a messaging app that is a favorite of the extreme right-wing, as well as criminals such as human traffickers, money launderers, and vendors of child pornography. As I write this in the fall of 2024, its founder is under investigation in France for his platform's failure to address these issues.

This list isn't complete! But it is a good starting place for concern. If your son is engaging with these content creators or using these platforms, you should be very concerned about the kind of media he's consuming—but that doesn't mean that these are the only platforms and content creators you should be concerned about! Much far-right content comes from sources you wouldn't expect: from video game streams, from private message boards, and from bigger social media sites like YouTube, TikTok, and Facebook. Wherever it comes from, the problem isn't just extreme right-wing media sources, but extreme right wing *messages*.

FIGURE 3.2 shows how seemingly innocuous starting points can lead to more fascist ones. A young person might start off hearing and telling racist, sexist, or

"It's just a joke!"	⇨	"People like me are the real victims."	⇨	White Supremacy, Male Supremacy
"I'm just asking questions!"	⇨	"Mainstream media is lying about this."	⇨	Only trusting conspiracy theories
"I feel spiritually and socially lost."	⇨	"Old traditions give answer and structure."	⇨	Liberal, tolerant society is the problem

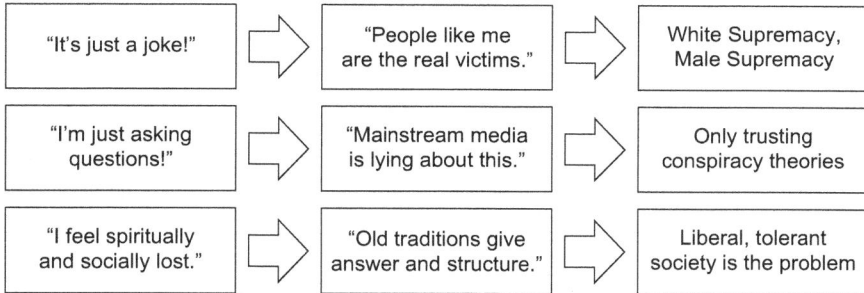

FIGURE 3.2   Here are some arguments your son, or anybody who's fallen in with the extreme right-wing, might use to push back against you or to justify their beliefs. They'll start with what might seem like a reasonable position, then could move to more and more radical ones.

Source: Author's creation.

homophobic jokes, excusing them as just humor that's harming nobody. People's reactions to those jokes could lead him to conclude that *he's* the real victim—he can't make the jokes he wants, and everyone is ganging up on him! From there, hundreds and thousands of voices online will tell him that modern society is *really* discriminating against young men just like him.

A more obviously political way into the right-wing could start with curiosity about a historical event like September 11, the Holocaust, or the US Civil War. Depending on the sources the young person encounters, they might find some that advocate for radical or unsupported positions related to conspiracy theories. Those theories will tell him that he can't trust any mainstream accounts about anything, which could lead to more disturbing forms of conspiratorial thinking, like arguing that Barack Obama or Kamala Harris is not eligible to be the President of the United States, anti-Semitism, or Holocaust denial.

Other young people might find their way to the extreme right-wing out of a crisis of spiritual or personal identity. This is a common experience in the modern world and is not isolated to the young! For many people, these questions are answered by going to a mainstream church, finding their own spiritual practice, or spending time in nature. But for others, they seek answers in old, established traditions: 19th-century or even medieval conservative Catholicism, the idea of Hindu practices before the arrival of Islam in India, etc. Alone, these aren't cause for concern, but they can lead a young person to conclude that if the answers are in the past, the present is the problem—specifically, the liberal, tolerant, diverse, democratic world that so many extreme right-wingers blame for all of their and all of society's problems.

I'll be coming back to this chart in the next chapter, talking about how to intervene in this kind of radicalization.

What You Can Do?

I want to close this chapter by giving you some more timeless guidelines for identifying youth radicalization. When it comes to general signs of right-wing radicalization or extremist tendencies in young men, there are clear signs you can keep an eye out for. These should help you whether you're reading this book a few months after it comes out or several years later, after the particular influencers and media personalities I've listed here have (hopefully) lost their power and influence.

What you should keep your eye on depends on your son's age, of course. Radicalization and extremist ideology come in many different forms, and since we're dealing with an age range that runs from preteen up through the early twenties, there are going to be some major differences in what you might notice and how you can respond to it.

Very young men, starting around age 10 to 12, will start to see increasingly radical content online or on whatever social media or communication platform is current for them. This was true when poorly copied pamphlets were the best means of mass communication, it was true for the radio, and it's true today with online and app-based radicalization. As I've noted elsewhere in this chapter, this will happen regardless of how you police or regulate your child's consumption of media content. As the right-wing becomes increasingly prevalent, its messaging is seeping into more and more mainstream products and content. You might restrict your son's use of the internet, but if some of the country's biggest music stars—such as Ye, formerly known as Kanye West—openly espouse anti-Semitic ideology, your son is simply going to hear about it.

If your son has never encountered these ideas before, he might be curious about them. It's possible that they'll spark his interest despite any effort on your part, simply because he's never heard people talk in such bigoted ways before. The right-wing tends to be incredibly reductive in its narratives, giving simple answers to incredibly complex questions—and unlike the left, which also does this but is open about the more complex logic that underlies its simple claims, the right-wing argues that reality just is that simple. Anti-Semitic logic, in particular, is a great tool for simplifying political narratives. It puts the blame at the feet of a specific group of people and argues that they're behind literally everything wrong that happens in the world.

After coming across this kind of compellingly simple ideology, your son might do a few different things. He might try some of this ideology on for size and see what will happen if he repeats some of its ideas in company. How would you or his teachers react if he mentioned these ideas? Children are curious and still learning how the world will respond to them, still testing boundaries and doing things more to provoke reactions than they're doing them because they really believe in what they're doing or saying.

So, when your son is young, the primary thing to watch out for is fairly sudden habit swings in media consumption or friend groups. If you're in the habit of talking to your son about his social life, it should be fairly easy for you to learn when your son's social circle has changed a lot. Ask him about his friends, ask him what they do together, and ask what they enjoy about each other's company. If his answers start to touch on the insensitive or off-color jokes they make, then you need to be on alert—but don't panic yet! Like I said, many kids around 12–20 go through periods of using inflammatory language or flippantly discussing complex topics as a means of rebelling. If you show your son that you only disapprove of his friends, rather than having a curious and questioning attitude toward them, it could make those people more interesting to him.

If your son's media consumption changes abruptly or alarmingly, you need to pay attention to whatever it is that he's now fixated on—and you need to be prepared to be surprised at the connections made between a lot of types of media and the right-wing. In previous generations, right-wing youth consumed right-wing media, like openly skinhead-oriented or openly racist bands. Today, that is less the case, with most young racists consuming the same music media that others do. There are even some shows, such as My Little Pony, that were originally marketed toward young women but have gained a strong audience of young men, many of them white supremacists and right-wing.

This means that if your son's media consumption changes rapidly, it likely won't be as easy as seeing that he's gotten into a band with a name like "Race War Now." Instead, it might look like him following a new YouTube star and repeating what that person says. It might look like him spending a lot of time on a particular social media or chat page—whether that's on 4chan, 8kun, Reddit, a Discord server, or some social media platform that doesn't exist as I'm writing this. When your son joins a new community or gets excited about a new form of content, it's your job to find out as much about it as you can. What does he like about this content? How does he relate to it?

These conversations might start very much like the ones I suggested having with your son over video games. You might start with questions like this:

- What do you like about these new friends?
- What do you talk about together?
- It sounds like these people make you laugh a lot. What do you laugh about together?

If your son is talking about memes or other online content, just ask him to share them with you. Do this in the same way that you might ask him to show you an episode of a show he likes or share a joking story he heard from a friend. If it turns out that this meme or content is problematic for some reason—maybe it uses a racial slur, maybe it's sexist, etc.—don't immediately blow up or start a conflict.

Instead, use this as an opportunity to get to know more about how your son engages with this content.

- I don't see that kind of stuff online—where did you come across it? A friend, message board, a Discord server, TikTok, etc.?
- I don't get the joke—can you tell me what's funny about this?
- When I hear that kind of thing, it makes me feel like this. How does it make you feel?

Essentially, you're trying to figure out how your son engages with problematic content. If your son has latched onto this content in the way that people from my generation appreciated something like South Park, which relies on irreverent humor and boundary-pushing concepts, then you can generally rest assured that while you might not approve of what your son is seeing or sharing, it isn't much more than adolescent boundary-pushing and risk ignorance. It'll be important for you to keep an eye on this stuff, since the right-wing often hides behind their propaganda being nothing but a "joke," but there's no need to panic just yet.

On the other hand, it's possible you'll learn from these conversations that your son has fallen a lot deeper down the rabbit hole. In that case, you'll need to use the resources and suggestions found in the next chapter to try to get your son out of it.

After reading this chapter, you should have a better idea of the ways that the right-wing uses online and in-person means of radicalization, and a better idea of why it is that the right-wing is growing in our world today. This is the end of the preparatory parts of the book, where I've talked about what fascism is and how we can understand it. Now I'll move on to the second half of the book; practical advice about how to deal with fascism in the life of your son, your community, and the world around you.

Notes

1 Thompson, Carolyn, "Prosecutors to Seek Death Penalty for White Supremacist Who Killed 10 at Buffalo Supermarket," *AP News*, January 12, 2024.
2 Ferguson, Christopher J., "Violent Video Games, Mass Shootings, and the Supreme Court: Lessons for the Legal Community in the Wake of Recent Free Speech Cases and Mass Shootings," *New Criminal Law Review: An International and Interdisciplinary Journal* 17, no. 4 (2014): 553–86.
3 Cote, Amanda C., *Gaming Sexism: Gender and Identity in the Era of Casual Video Games*. New York: New York University Press, 2020. https://doi.org/10.18574/nyu/978147983 8523.001.0001.
4 Wendling, Mike, "Accused Pelosi Hammer Attacker David DePape Tearfully Testifies of Bizarre Plot," *BBC*, November 15, 2023.
5 Paul, Christopher A., "A Toxic Culture: Studying Gaming's Jerks," in *The Toxic Meritocracy of Video Games: Why Gaming Culture Is the Worst*. Minneapolis: University of Minnesota Press, 2018. Pg 63–90; Poland, Bailey, *Haters: Harassment, Abuse, and Violence Online*. Lincoln, NE: University of Nebraska Press, 2016.

6 Hern, Alex, "PewDiePie: YouTube Megastar's N-Word Outburst Sparks Developer Backlash," *BBC*, September 11, 2017.

7 Choski, Niraj, "PewDiePie Put in Spotlight After New Zealand Shooting," *The New York Times*, March 15, 2019. The phrase "subscribe to PewDiePie" was a reference to a then-ongoing online rivalry between Kjellberg and the Indian media company T-Series.

8 For more on this, check out the Southern Poverty Law Center's "Year in Hate and Extremism Report," which has a lengthy section on "pick up artists" and their connections to extremism.

9 In addition to the organizations I've already referenced in this book, there are dozens— maybe even hundreds—of organizations that pay attention to it. There are progressive groups like Political Research Associates, as well as more conservative ones like the McCain Foundation, and government offices like the Working Group to Counter Online Radicalization to Violence out of the United States's Department of Justice.

10 For examples of their rhetoric, see www.tpusa.com.

4

HOW TO TALK TO YOUR SON ABOUT FASCISM

Approaching talking to your son about fascism from a place of humility and care will go a long way in helping you and your son deal with these issues together. Talking to your son about fascism will be as difficult as talking to him about any other sensitive topic he might have encountered elsewhere in life, such as sex, gender, bullying, or pornography. You can and should use the skills you've developed in addressing those subjects to broach this one.

But there are some key differences between those conversations and talking with your son about fascism. The first is that, unlike with sex, gender, dating, bullying, pornography, or drugs, you very likely didn't grow up in an environment where fascism and extreme right-wing messaging was a subject of concern. We're currently living through one of the biggest surges of fascist messaging and growth since WWII. This means that you and your son can't rely on the assumption that you, as a parent, have experiences you can draw on to help him through. If you feel like you're in uncharted territory, that's why.

The other major difference between the standard parent-kid conversations and this one is that this one is about politics. It's about something that your son will have to make up his own mind about, one way or another—an adult subject that people disagree over and handle differently. This means that you have to approach these conversations not as someone who's laying down the law and telling him what to do, like what level of dating or drug use you're comfortable with. Acting that way in a conversation about fascism will only make rebelling against your rules more exciting. Instead, you need to approach this conversation as someone who is working *with* him to do something good and important together.

Fascism is a part of the adult world. Exposure to some of the right-wing perspectives that are discussed earlier in this book might be the first time your son feels like someone is talking to him like an adult about politics. That's one of the

DOI: 10.4324/9781003385509-5

insidious things about the far-right's use of the internet to recruit young men. Like I said in Chapters 2 and 3, it relies on them being just old enough to think about political matters but not yet allowed to participate in them. Joining right-wing communities is an opportunity for that kind of belonging, engagement, and a feeling of importance.

One of the challenges you'll face while talking with your son about fascism will be the same as with other parenting challenges—that you'll need to be on the same page as everyone else who is parenting your son. This includes a spouse, if you have one, but also any former spouses or step-parents who might be in the picture, as well as close relatives, chosen family, or anyone else your son might look to for moral guidance. Having a united front on fascism is just as important as having a common policy on drug use, pornography, dating, or any other tricky subject that deals with how young people navigate the road to adulthood.

Another reason talking to your son about fascism will be hard is that it is embarrassing. You might find it difficult to discuss some of the worst things that human beings have done. People are understandably reluctant to introduce these terrible ideas into their children's lives, and I get why they might think it'd be better to just avoid the subject and hope their kids don't encounter it. The sad truth is that these beliefs are out there. Your son *will* encounter them, whether online or in person. The difference you can make is whether he hears about fascism for the first time from you, having read this book and prepared him to deal with it as an adult, or from a friend egging him on and making it seem cool or edgy.

Lastly, talking to your son about fascism will be uncomfortable because it'll force you to confront your own behavior and language. If you use sexist, ableist, gendered, or racist slurs or terms, it might be difficult to criticize your son for doing so. If you laugh at jokes that you're encouraging him to question, he might not be able or willing to understand if you're doing so ironically or out of nostalgia for an old TV show or comedian you grew up liking. You can use this as an opportunity to work on this behavior for yourself if this self-reflection leads to behaviors you want to change.

I encourage you to lean into the discomfort of talking to your son about fascism. If you're uncomfortable with it, scared by it, or emotionally affected by it, share that with your son. It'll help him see how serious this topic is and that you're trusting him with something serious by talking about it with him.

Fighting Fascism at Home

What I'm about to tell you to do to stop your son from becoming a fascist flies in the face of most advice about how to deal with the extreme right-wing. Most commentators and observers will tell you that you need to keep fascism from speaking or from taking up any space at all—I'm going to tell you to listen to and engage with your son. Most people will tell you that fascism should be either directly attacked or laughed at—I'm going to tell you to take your son's thoughts seriously.

Most people will tell you that you need to consider physically attacking fascists when they appear in public—I'm going to tell you to be extremely careful about punishing your son for curiosity or interest he might show in fascist or right-wing topics.

This position is uncomfortable for me. I am a proud antifascist. I consider fascism to be one of the most dangerous ideologies that human beings have ever produced. I've dedicated my adult life to studying, understanding, and combating it. I agree with the wisdom that fascism needs to be openly fought if we're going to stop it from growing and eventually taking power in our society. So why am I telling you to be kind, thoughtful, and a good listener, when my instinct is to tell you to close yourself off to any and all right-wing messaging?

The answer is obvious, but I've still needed to remind myself of it constantly while writing this book. It's because this isn't a book about how to stop fascism in the streets or in government. There are many other excellent guides about how to do that.[1] Instead, this is a book about how to deal with fascism in *private*—in the home, at school, in church, in a community organization, in a chat group, and amongst friends.

Academics describe the difference between these two parts of our lives as belonging to the public sphere or the private sphere. In public, we're anonymous statistics, part of crowds and voting blocs, just one person in a trend or a group. In private, we're individuals with feelings and specific relationships whose politics probably don't conform exactly to our demographic data. Think about it as the difference between a news story about changing poll numbers and one where the reporter goes to a restaurant in rural Alabama to talk to people—they do that because they're hoping to get the perspectives of actual people rather than the very broad brushstrokes they'd get with a survey.

People act differently in the public and private spheres. In private, they might be kind to everyone they meet, but in public, they might vote to deprive people of the right to food or deny them adequate education. In public, they might support racially discriminatory policies, but in private, they might fall in love with a person of a different race. Getting your friend to stop using a sexist term in private is entirely different from getting them to vote for candidates that support women's rights, for example.

Fighting fascism is no different. The ways that we can fight fascism in public life versus in private life are so different as to be almost opposite. In public, fascists are anonymous threats. In private, they're people you might know and love. In public, fascists need to be silenced. In private, as long as they're not actively hurting anyone, the best way to change their minds is to talk to them and try to get at the root of what's driving them to this ideology. In public, fascism needs to be fought, sometimes physically. In private, altercation and especially violence will do nothing but drive your son further away from you and the other people in his life who could stop him from becoming a full-fledged fascist.

Chapter 6 covers public-facing ways to fight fascism. It has guides for how you can build on the antifascist connection you and your son are developing to help fight fascism in your local community, your city, and your country. It'll tell you how to confront it with your voice, your vote, and if it's safe, with your body. But you won't be able to do that well without having built a strong, personal connection with your son focused on fighting fascism together—and that means first fighting fascism in the private sphere.

The key to talking to your son about fascism is the same as it is for any other thorny, difficult issue—you need to express compassion and empathy for what your son is going through and the feelings he is experiencing. The worst thing you could do when your son is expressing an interest in the right-wing is to show disgust or shun him. Instead, as a parent, you have to try your best to allow him to express himself and his interests while providing a safe set of boundaries to keep him away from the real dangers he faces.

Having empathy for your son *does not* mean having empathy for fascism. I am not telling you to seriously consider fascist or other extreme right-wing perspectives. Your empathy is for your son, not for his beliefs.

Like I discussed in Chapter 3, many young men will encounter extremist ideology just because of the kind of online and in-person environments they inhabit Because these things are popular among young people, platforms and algorithms will encourage them to see it and will reward them for consuming it by pushing them further down that same rabbit hole. Most of these young men will end up repeating this content to their friends and peers the same way they might repeat a joke from a show or video game or tell a story that will make people laugh. They literally don't know what they're talking about.

I have a friend who works in secondary education. His job is primarily disciplinary—he's the guy the kids see when they've made a mistake or when they've done something cruel. He says that all too often, when a teenager comes into his office having done something wrong, like calling someone a racial slur, physically hitting someone, or making fun of a student or faculty member, they seem just as confused as he is about why they're there. He'll ask them why they did what they did, and most of the time they'll answer, "I don't know." Most of the time, he answers back, "I believe you."

My friend is no fool. He can tell when kids are just hiding their motivations and trying not to get caught. It's just that much of the time, adolescents, teenagers, and young men are acting out for reasons that don't really make sense to them when they stop and think about it. They're testing options or trying to fit in, or they're just acting impulsively in a way that older people just can't really understand anymore because our brains have changed. That doesn't condone their actions or mean that they won't get punished for them. But it does mean that some empathy might be in order.

Parenting With Empathy

Aside from the book you're reading right now, there's no guide for parents who are trying to keep their kids out of the right-wing. What we do have are a lot of books that are about how to keep your kid out of a gang, or how to stop them from getting into dangerous drug consumption habits, or how to stop them from exhibiting racial or gender bias. We can build on some of these same strategies to help us keep kids from becoming fascists.

If you read the popular parenting books on the market today, you'll find them divided over the subject of how to discipline and motivate your children. Many of the more conservative, older books focus on creating a functional "consultant" relationship with your child so that when the time comes, you're still firmly the one in charge.

There is something useful in this perspective, especially when it comes to fascism and the right-wing. It likely won't help you to get into a knock-down, drag-out fight with your teenager over the merits of Andrew Tate, Nick Fuentes, or whoever the right-wing provocateur of the hour is when you're reading this book. As I've said before, that's really most likely to turn your son away from you rather than help him see the error of his ways.

But the attitude they suggest you adopt is one of someone who always knows better, every single time. While that might have been the case when your son was five, and possibly even when he's ten, it'll stop being so useful when your son is a teenager or a young man. A major part of what I hope you get from this book is understanding and accepting that your son's political opinions are his and his alone—not only are there moral problems with telling your son he's not allowed to believe one thing or another, but it's just not likely to actually get him to move in the direction you want.

Instead, you need to take these conversations as an opportunity to invite adult behavior from your son and to model the same back at him in your conversations. You can show him that while some people yell and scream and make a scene when they talk about politics, he doesn't have to. Instead, he can follow your example and talk about the facts and his opinions with respect and care. Model that behavior for him when you talk to him about fascism.

This tactic has two main benefits. The first is that it's likely the best way for you to get buy-in from your son when it comes to listening and talking to you about his political opinions. Despite what the anger in your body wants you to believe, people rarely listen when they're being yelled at. Second, and more importantly, it will force your son to carefully consider his thoughts before sharing them with you. If you engage in an earnest conversation that examines both of your perspectives, it's unlikely that he'll feel attacked or called out for what he's saying, which is a recipe for him retreating to an echo chamber.

Now this advice might get me in some trouble with some other people who are dedicated to stopping the rise of the right-wing. Most people who focus on fighting the extreme right-wing will tell you that the correct way to combat their speech is to have a "no quarter" approach. You need to deny fascism any space and constantly push them back to the fringe. Fascists often take advantage of supposedly earnest debates by engaging in them with no intention of re-examining their positions and with no desire to consider their opponent's perspectives. For that reason, it's generally useless to debate them in this way. I agree with this approach wholeheartedly, and I'll get back to it in the last chapter of this book.

But things are different when we're talking about debating or talking with your own son. You, as a parent and caretaker, are in a unique position with your son, a young man who's developing an interest in fascist or right-wing thinking. You might be one of the only people in his life who can sympathize with his feelings and experiences without agreeing with him or condoning his behavior.

This is why, unlike anybody else, it might be beneficial for you to sit down and listen to your son's thoughts about race relations, or gender disparities he might consider "unfair," or any number of other things he might think that don't merit the time of the people whom those opinions oppress or hurt.

Age Matters When Talking to Your Son About Fascism

Of course, the age of your son plays a massive role in how you should talk to him about fascism. There's a massive difference between the kind of conversation you'd have with a 12-year-old or a 22-year-old.

The way you explain fascism to your son will depend on his age, just like any other parenting decisions and discussions you may have. For a very young son, it might be enough for him to understand that fascists are the villains of the stories they're included in—they're the people Indiana Jones beats at the end of the day, and they're the people chasing the protagonists in *Number the Stars*. Someone younger than a teenager is probably not capable of the kind of systematic thinking needed to understand fascism as a social threat rather than a merely personal one. It's OK if your young son comes away from learning about fascism only understanding that it's something that bad people did in the past, in the same way that he couldn't understand that enslavement built the United States, only that it's wrong and something terrible that happened over a hundred years ago.

The thing you need to make sure your son understands is that just because the Nazis and the Italian Fascists were defeated in the war, that doesn't mean that fascists are gone. His history classes in school will probably not teach him this. In the same way that the US South lost, but many people still have their prejudices, many millions of people all around the world still agree with those historical politicians and leaders. This might be the most that a ten-year-old can handle.

A student in middle school is entering the age when they're ready to hear about fascism as something that's part of the world around them right now. Just as they're starting to hear about political messages on their own and are on the cusp of being voters themselves, they'll need to start to understand fascism as a real and living force in politics today. For these preteen and teenage sons, you'll need to strike a balance between explaining fascism's past with enough detail that it accurately represents what happened and not overwhelming them with so much information that it sounds like just another bad thing that happened.

This is an age at which your son is probably the most susceptible to peer pressure that he'll ever be. No longer just a kid, who might more easily accept what his parents say, but not yet an adult, capable of coming to his own conclusions, these early years of adolescence are a time when a lot of young people find themselves interested in alternative lifestyles. Many of these are harmless or even positive, but others are downright dangerous. Fascism and the right-wing are one such example.

Talking to a middle school or high school-aged son about fascism means acknowledging grisly details without dwelling on them to the point of being frightening. Don't make this a lecture! Instead, ask your son what he's already heard about fascism. He might just talk about what he's learned in school, maybe from WWII. Or his answers might surprise you. He might know a lot about fascist governments in the past from playing a video game. Or he might have encountered right-wing content online that told him some false versions of right-wing history and politics.

Whatever he might have already heard, it's your job to listen to him and express empathy and interest in what he says. He might have an interest in fascism, or Nazis, or the US Civil War, or something else that you find distasteful—this probably isn't because he's already in the clutches of the right-wing. It's more likely that he's only interested in these things because they are taboo, or even because he's scared of them. Do your best to pick up on what he's expressing. Ask him outright why he's interested in these topics, and what he finds curious or compelling about them. Like many young men, he might be drawn to the grisly details, or to stories of war and hardship, rather than to the politics themselves.

More likely than not, though, your son won't express an opinion or have an interest in fascism or the right-wing. He'll probably blow it off in the same way that a teenager or young adult would blow off any other serious topic you might bring up—either out of disinterest or not wanting to be bogged down in a tough conversation with his parents. That means you'll have to start the conversation, and you'll be in the driver's seat for it.

Here are some conversation starters:

- Ask your son if he's heard of fascism or the right-wing. Ask him what he knows about it—and if he knows it's not just something from a history book but is something that people believe today too.
- If (or, sadly, when) something terrible and related to fascism happens in the world, ask him what he knows and what he's heard about it. If there's been a mass shooting motivated by white supremacist ideology, or if a major extreme right-wing party has won an election, ask him what he knows about them. He might know a whole lot! Or he might know relatively little.
- When you watch a movie, hear something on the radio, or see a video that deals with fascism, ask him if he knows what they're talking about. Ask him to explain it back to you, in the same way you might ask him to show you that he understands some homework you're helping him with.

- If your son shares right-wing content with you—a joke or a meme, for example—ask him where he saw it. Ask him to explain what he finds interesting, funny, or compelling about it.

However you start the conversation, you have to be sure that your son thinks of you as someone he can feel safe expressing curiosity around. Your job is to come across as knowledgeable but open to listening. Don't claim to have all the answers. If you approach talking about fascism and the right-wing as a team, then he'll be more likely to trust you in the future.

But no matter how curious and accepting of your son you are, you also have to be sure that your son comes away from the conversation knowing that you have some hard limits. He needs to know that you don't accept or agree with fascism, and why. This is a good time to share your own experiences and perspective, and why you're concerned about fascism. Talk about your own feelings—how the rise of fascism makes you angry or scared, and how it might affect you or people you love and care about. You want to be sure that he comes away from the conversation knowing that you disagree with fascism, and not just in a "I don't like mayonnaise" kind of way. It needs to be clear that you think fascism is dangerous, and that while you love and respect him, you'd be very worried and concerned if he were to turn to the extreme right-wing. At this stage, avoid ultimatums.

Talking to a tween or teen about fascism means balancing treating him as a young adult with still being a parental, caretaking figure. Show your son that you're starting to trust him as an independent person while you're still there to catch him if he falls.

If your son is older, for example, nearing the end of high school or in college, then you will need to relate to him as an adult when it comes to politics. From a legal and arguably moral standpoint, it's no longer your responsibility what he believes, how he votes, or what kind of political company he keeps. Still, you're hopefully concerned about what he thinks and how he lives in the world, and you want to help influence him away from the right-wing.

Ask him about his opinion and treat him like an equal. If he says something you disagree with, tell him. If he says or does something bigoted or wrong, treat it like you would if your best friend had done it. Talk through your concerns and disagreements.

Young adulthood will be the most dangerous time for the right-wing radicalization of the young men in your life—while many people who've participated in right-wing violence were radicalized at a younger age, the majority of violence is committed by men who are college-aged. This is partly simply due to access to weapons, but it's also a function of their role in fascist organizations at this age. Young adult men, legal adults but still impressionable and still early recruits to their organizations, are impressionable and more easily motivated to participate in serious acts of violence. Men at this age are the foot soldiers, doing the dirty work of right-wing leaders who are generally older or middle-aged.

As always, my advice to you is that no matter how fascism and the extreme right-wing come up—whether from the news, a piece of media, or anywhere else—start from a place of curiosity and empathy. Ask your son what he thinks and where he stands. Ask him how he gets his news and where his sources come from. Ask him what his friends say and if that depends on their race, gender, or sexuality. Share experiences you've had with friends who express these beliefs.

Since your son is older, you can't be a parent in the same way you used to be. You can't limit his behavior, and you can't tell him what to do. Instead, you have to treat him like an adult.

Just like you would with any other adult, express your opinion and disapproval of fascism and the extreme right-wing when it's relevant. If your son answers back that he's on the same page, good! He might have gotten there himself, or you might've parented and directed him away from the right-wing with some of the techniques in this book. In any case, a lot of your work is already done. There are still some things you might want to check in on, like whether he knows the connection between some popular influencers or something in the news and the extreme right-wing. You'll still want to keep an eye on a young man in his late teens to early twenties, as that is still the most dangerous time for right-wing recruitment and activity.

Things might be harder if he shows an interest in fascism, but you can still follow much the same advice. If you disagree with something he said, tell him. If you don't believe something he's said without presenting evidence, ask for it before you keep going. Show him that you care about him and that his opinion matters to you by taking it seriously and debating him just as you would anybody else. If your son is already showing a worrying interest in the right-wing, or it seems like he's actually involved in fascist activity, check out some of the guides I've included later in this chapter for how to address those concerns.

Here are some conversation examples:

- Your son says that he supports an openly white-supremacist politician. Tell him that you disagree with him completely, and tell him why. Ask him why he supports this politician. Debate him calmly and as an adult.
- Your son complains that he can't get a girlfriend or that dating is hard or impossible now for people like him (he might mean this due to his race, his physical appearance, etc.). Ask him what he means, and listen closely to his response. If he sounds like he's expressing general angst and disappointment, then move from there. But if he seems to be blaming women *in general* for not getting a date or blaming another ethnic group for his inability to date, check in. Ask him where he got those ideas.
- Your son tells a sexist joke. Tell him that now that he's an adult you're treating him like one and that you don't want to be around people who think that kind of thing is funny. Ask him what he finds funny about it.

- You learn that your son has joined a right-wing organization or that he's engaging with right-wing content online. Treat this the same way you'd treat learning that your son has a problem with a hard drug—this is a time to both show love and set boundaries. Tell him that you won't have any part in the activities or ideology of this group and that you won't support him while he's involved in it. Remind him that you love him and that you're always there to talk, but that you won't be a sounding board for beliefs that are so harmful.

If, or when, your son says or does something that connects to the extreme right-wing, you shouldn't push him away. Instead, embrace him and help him learn from what he's done. Activists and educators are beginning to call this approach "calling in" rather than "calling out." When you call out bad behavior, teens and adolescents learn that they aren't accepted in their community and seek alternatives. When you call them in instead, they learn that they can make mistakes and that you trust they are still growing and changing, that they have space and opportunity to learn from their past.

Prevention

When it comes to fascism, an ounce of prevention is worth a pound of cure. It's much better and much easier to work to avoid the radicalization of your son than it would be to de-radicalize him if he were to actually become a fascist. Studies show that it is massively harder to dig someone out of an ideological hole than to keep them from falling in! The earlier you can start, the better.

When it comes to helping your kids deal with extremism online, experts agree that "there's really nothing that compares to intervention before they come across the video or content. There's nothing better than early intervention," says Étienne Quintal of CIVIX. "We need to be better at speaking to kids about this stuff early on, before they see it for themselves." Just the same way that you might talk to your children about sex and gender before they've reached puberty, the time to talk to them about fascism and the right-wing is long before they start forming their own political opinions.

You've got to talk to your kids about hate, conspiracy theories, and racism, you've got to get your head out of the sand and understand that this isn't a problem we're going to have to deal with in the future—it's a problem that already exists. But if we give them the tools they need to notice this stuff early on, then when they do see it they can understand it for what it is.

As I mentioned in a previous chapter, your first instinct in keeping your son away from right-wing messaging might be to try to restrict his media consumption in order to prevent him from seeing any right-wing content at all. If you only curated your son's social and media environment, then he couldn't be radicalized, right?

The issue is that you need to think about what that really means. It would mean having an extremely robust system of online protections that goes far beyond the standard set, which is usually oriented around pornography rather than any other kind of dangerous or disturbing content. Even those filters are woefully inadequate, since they rely on a list of website addresses rather than a robust system of evaluating the nature of any site individually. In order to fully block your son from encountering hateful or radicalizing content online, you'd need to restrict him to only using his browser and certain approved apps and have an extremely complete understanding of all the online sites and sources of that content. Maintaining lists like that is many people's full-time jobs, and even they have a hard time keeping track of it all. This has only been exacerbated by the elimination of much of the content monitoring that took place via social media staff, for example, after Elon Musk's acquisition of Twitter.[2] Keeping this content away from your son also means staying on top of the apps and websites that are popular among young people, itself a monumental and ever-changing task.

This doesn't mean that some level of protective monitoring is useless. If this is something you'd like to install on your son's phone or computer, or potentially on all internet devices in your home, take a look online or in the app store for you and your son's phones. I advise you to be careful pursuing an option like this—as I said in Chapter 3, it runs the risk of making fascism and the far right seem more appealing because they've been made taboo. And the fact is that even the most robust filters and censorship can't keep up with right-wing culture or online culture in general.

The most important thing you can do with your son's media taste is to show curiosity and humility. "If you can start early with your kid, if you're a parent who can show curiosity about their media use and have those conversations on an equal level, then you're ahead of the curve," says Dimitri Pavlounis of CIVIX. "It's much easier to start that dialogue with a kid at 8 than it is at 14." This should come as no surprise to those of you who are parents of teenagers, but they're reluctant to talk about most things in their lives. If you start earlier and show genuine interest in your son's tastes, it'll be more natural and normal for him to come to you when he sees extremist content and wants to talk about it—and it'll be more natural for it to come up in conversation if you're regularly asking him what kind of media he's seeing and consuming.

Let's imagine a bad scenario. Your son repeats something from the internet that he's seen or heard, and it sounds to you like hate speech. Maybe he's made an anti-Semitic joke, or mentioned a racist trope, or casually talked about sex and gender roles in a sexist or homophobic way. If you've never spoken to your son about these things before, or if you've only talked to him about them as a lecture, then reprimanding him will likely not solve the problem. Instead of learning that what he just said is wrong or problematic, he'll just learn to hide it from you. He'll also learn that the people in power over him don't like what he's said or what he thinks, which is the foundation of a lot of conspiratorial thinking. That means that you need to approach the conversation from a place of empathy and interest, even if you are already certain of your own opinion on these issues and the content your son is talking about.

The issue is that from an institutional level, "most of the time, when a student has made a misogynist comment, it might be too late for that person," says Dimitri That's why prevention plays such a big role in their discussions.

So, if you can't effectively keep your son away from this content online, what if you just kept him offline entirely? That would certainly make it harder for him to access hateful and radicalizing messages. But studies show that this is also a dead end. Either you and everyone else in your family would have to be completely offline—with no computers or internet-capable devices present in the home at all—or you'd need exactly the same kind of protections that I've just noted can't do the job well enough to keep radicalizing content away from young men. We might dream of a day when access to the internet isn't necessary for personal advancement, but sadly that is a fair bit in the future.

And even *if* you did keep your son (and your family) offline or somehow accumulated the right collection of software and apps that would keep your son from seeing fascist content, there's still every chance for your son to encounter it in the real world too. As I discussed in the last chapter, fascism and the far-right grew long before the internet. Unless you move your family to a fully isolated rural community with exclusively like-minded people, your son will encounter the right-wing at some point in his development.

What's worse, this kind of prevention-by-deprivation will likely only make your son more curious about the content you're keeping from him. Whatever generation you belong to, you remember the allure of the topics the adults stopped talking about when you entered the room, the channels they switched off when they saw you watching, the websites they told you to avoid or kept your browser from accessing, jokes they told you weren't funny, and books they were skeptical of you reading. If you were anything like me, like most other young people, the way adults treated this media only made you more curious about it, even fixated on it.

The worst thing you can do with a young man who's interested in fascism is to make it cool by making it taboo. That means you can't look away from it or avoid talking about it—you need to address the issue head-on. Because whether it's from a book, social media, a history class, a fellow young person, or online, your son *will* see right-wing messaging that is directed at him. It's your job to give him the tools he'll need to turn away from it on his own.

Young men whose brains are literally wired to encourage them to take increasing risks are simply more likely than their older peers to accept dangerous "assignments" from political superiors. This is why we see young men disproportionately engaging in street crime and political violence throughout the history of the right-wing—they're simply generally more willing to take those risks for the group. Organizations like the Proud Boys, or the various "active clubs" that mask their right-wing politics in supposedly being organized for the purposes of social-izing as physically active men, recruit young men who are eager for physical chal-lenges and bodily daring.

This daring is part of the real appeal of fascism for the young—it demands violence and action from young men whose bodies and brains are already primed for this behavior. Some people even argue that fascism's twin obsessions with masculinity and violence stem from this same root, that it is an ideology based in male psychochemistry. Being careful not to reduce a political ideology to simple biology, it is true that of the major modern political ideologies, fascism is the most immediate, illogical (in that it's opposed to logical reasoning), and prone to violence, which put together are a pretty good description of a teenage boy or young man.

We have our work cut out for us when it comes to dissuading them from joining groups that appeal to their desire for risk and danger. The pull of fascist violence and dangerous activity is one of the main reasons that it can be hard to keep fascism from being "cool" for young men. Instead, we need to offer alternatives that are equally appealing—as anyone who's tried to get a reluctant kid to eat vegetables instead of a cookie knows, it's not enough to tell them that it'll be good for them! You need to appeal to them in a way that makes sense to them.

Some of the skills you've already used to talk to your son about drugs and sex will be useful here. Sitting down with your son and having "the talk" is generally frowned on these days, as it tends to make the conversation in question awkward and forced. Instead, most psychologists and parenting sources suggest structuring these conversations as a series of smaller talks rather than a single big one. This not only takes the pressure off you to cover all possible content and questions in a single leap, but it also makes sure that your son doesn't feel too overwhelmed or confronted. Instead of being cornered by their parents to have a "serious talk," it's a set of smaller, more casual ones about a single aspect of sex or drugs, such as using contraceptives or the difference between legal and hard drugs.

Talking to your son about fascism should be the same. Rather than sitting down for one hours-long lecture that runs from Mussolini to MAGA, make sure that talking about politics and how it impacts real people is part of your everyday life. I know that for many people, this is the very last thing you want to do—to actively bring the far-right into your dinner table conversation. But I promise you, as a his-torian and as someone who has dedicated his life to fighting the right-wing, that it is necessary. Ignoring the problem will not make it go away.

You could start these conversations by asking your son what he's learned about fascism and the right-wing in his classes or from other sources. This is an oppor-tunity to listen—there's every chance your son knows something you don't, either because he figured it out after you left school or because he's gained some outside knowledge. Don't be alarmed if he knows a thing or two about fascism. This *could* be a sign of an early interest, or it could come from any number of popular video games that deal with fascism, or it could just be that you've got a young history buff on your hands.

Whatever your son knows or doesn't know about fascism, be sure he comes away from the conversation knowing that you consider it to be dangerous.

Alongside this, you need to talk to your son about what's happening in the world today. Ask him what he's heard about politicians like Donald Trump or whichever leading right-wing figure in your country is (Trump possibly being the most globally known). Again, this is an opportunity to listen, and not just because that's the best practice when parenting a kid, teen, or young adult. You should be curious about what your son thinks of these figures. He might know next to nothing, or it might turn out that he's been following the news, reading posts, or watching TikToks about them for months or years. You won't know until you ask!

The most important thing in these conversations is to have them *together*.

Bill Smith agrees with what most other experts say—the vital thing is providing kids who are interested in the right-wing with alternatives, especially alternative communities. "The first thing we need to do is create a community for young men where they feel like they can grow, and then also have the ability to challenge and not normalize patriarchy and toxic views." But this community can't feel like a punishment or a demand—it has to be organic, normal, and welcoming to the young men who join it. He jokes that this would work best if it came from a source that young men already trust—"If I could pick one group of people to instantly convert to the cause, to instantly be fighting against hatred and toxicity, it'd be football coaches."

But since we can't just change the culture of masculinity all at once, the best thing we can do is model positive masculinity for young men. My friend tries to do this in his work.

> Modeling good masculinity is really important to me. Early on, my goal was to project as much as possible that toxicity and bias weren't OK in my classroom. I would get upset and even angry when a kid did something toxic or terrible. I might've even snapped or said, "What the hell did you just say?"

The problem is that responding in that way, meeting their toxicity with aggression, isn't a good way to get people to change their behavior in the long term, at least not if you want them to change out of a desire to be better instead of a desire not to get punished. You have to start "calling them in" rather than "calling them out."

You won't be alone in helping keep your son out of fascism. There are dozens of organizations throughout the United States, Canada, and the United Kingdom that help young men dealing with the right-wing, and with right-wing messaging they're seeing in their everyday lives. Many of these organizations are preventative—that is, their goal is to help people stay away from fascism and the right-wing before they get too involved. Some of these organizations are educational and work in classrooms and other community spaces to give kids the tools they need to avoid fascism without mentioning it by name. Others are more focused and specifically talk to kids about fascism and the right-wing.

- In the United States, there's Life After Hate, a nonprofit organization whose goal is to provide people with an offramp from hateful activity and thinking. It's received some funding from the US government but remains an independent organization.
- Formers Anonymous is a 12-step program—like Alcoholics Anonymous—that focuses on people who are former members of extremist organizations helping each other through getting away from that lifestyle and community.
- In the United Kingdom, Germany, and the Scandinavian countries, there are several groups under the EXIT umbrella. These organizations link up people who are involved with extremism to mentors, educators, and former extremists to help them transition to normal life. They also provide resources for family members of those who have gotten caught up in the right-wing.

But you should also be cautious about these organizations. When I spoke to Joan Braune, a scholar who studies radicalization and de-radicalization, she expressed concern about these groups and their efficacy. "The issue with some of these groups," she said, "is that they can lead to you spending more time with people connected to the right-wing than you otherwise would have." The comparison here is with "Scared Straight" programs, which were intended to frighten young people away from crime by having them go into jails and talk to prisoners. Braune told me that data shows these programs have had the opposite effect—people who go into "Scared Straight" programs actually have higher rates of incarceration and contact with police than their peers who didn't.

Braune shares similar cautions about many groups that claim to be working against the radicalization of young men. "If you're too nice to these people, if you end up palling around with them, then you can wind up enabling them," she says. Instead, you have to walk a very fine line between meeting people where they're and making it clear that there are some perspectives you won't engage with at all. Still, if you're someone who's influential in someone's life, then you can work with them honestly and try to help lead them away from their ideology.

She suggests taking their concerns and ideas seriously, and being willing to talk about difficult subjects like race and religion, but also about philosophy and history. "A lot of young men come to the right-wing looking for meaning," she says. Often, the right-wingers are the first people who've talked to them about serious issues as if their opinion mattered. It's your job to do the same thing, and to stop them from falling further down the right-wing rabbit hole.

When Prevention Doesn't Work

It's possible that you're reading this book because your son has already expressed fascist views, or even done something that indicates his interest in fascism. If that is your situation, I want to start by saying that I'm sorry you're dealing with this. Many parents don't anticipate their children behaving in this way and are blind-sided by this experience. That's a perfectly reasonable way to feel!

I also want to remind you about what was discussed in the first chapters. Fascism is unfortunately very common, and it appeals to a lot of young men in different countries and at different times. If your son has taken an interest in the extreme right-wing, it doesn't mean that there's something wrong with you, your family, or your parenting. Fascism is a part of our society, and it's sadly normal for some young men to be interested in it. Blaming yourself will not help you, your son, or the rest of us who want there to be fewer fascist young men.

There are some obvious warning signs that your son might be gaining an inter-est in fascism and the far right. I'd imagine that you don't need me or this book to tell you that if you see your son reading *Mein Kampf* or hanging a swastika flag in his bedroom, he might be gaining an interest in the right-wing! But there are other warning signs that might be less obvious to you. Some of these include:

- Sudden changes in the friends he spends time with
- Sudden changes in media consumption, especially if that media consumption swings in the direction of things enjoyed by the right-wing
- Changes in how he talks to or talks about women or people of color
- Mentioning right-wing media outlets or right-wing influencers, not just out of curiosity but out of interest and potential agreement
- A desire to pursue a violent sport or martial art when he had no interest in that before
- A sudden fascination with military history or with video games that deal with military history or military action

To be clear, these aren't necessarily indicators of your son being fascist, or even that he's connecting with the extreme right-wing! Instead, they're signs that your son is interested in or pursuing connection with cultures and subcultures that are often gateways to the right. The online and in-person sources of right-wing ideol-ogy discussed in Chapter 3 are useful to review here.

FIGURE 4.1 is another version of a chart I showed you in the previous chapter, showing how young men can get sucked into right-wing ideologies starting from innocuous places. This time, I've included offramps for those conversations. If

"It's just a joke!"	"People like me are the real victims."	White Supremacy, Male Supremacy
"I don't understand what's funny about that."	Open, discussion of privilege	
"I'm just asking questions!"	"Mainstream media is lying about this."	Only trusting conspiracy theories
"Let's research it together."	Go through the points one by one	
"I feel spiritually and socially lost."	"Old traditions give answer and structure."	Liberal, tolerant society is the problem
Empathize! Help with community and belonging	"What about the people they leave behind?"	

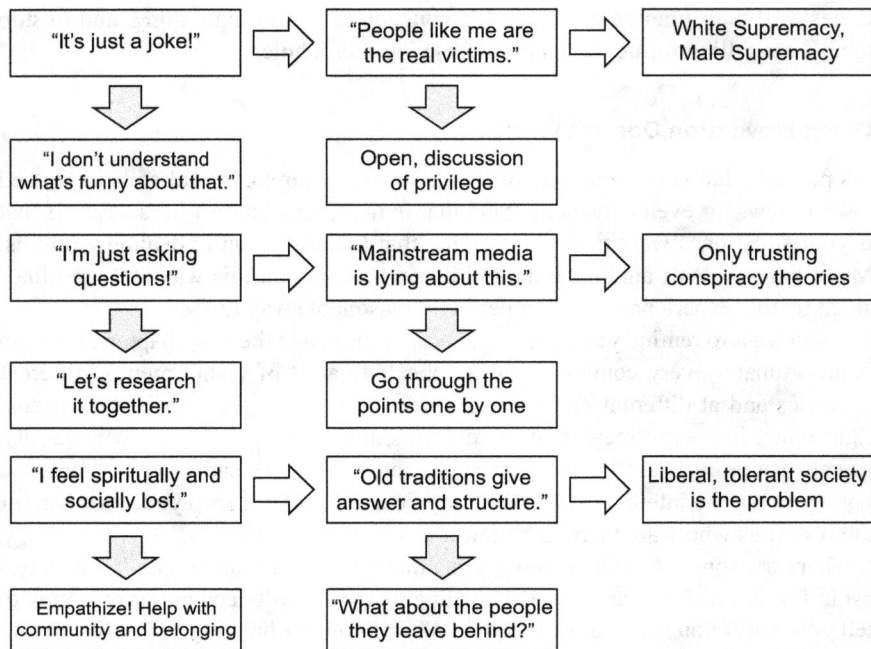

FIGURE 4.1 This chart returns to Figure 3.2 from the previous chapter and shows how you might intervene *before* things get too serious.

Source: Author's creation.

your son is "just making jokes," tell him you don't think they're funny and why. Don't confront him—that'll only drive him further away. Ask him what's funny about them. If he starts to show signs that he feels like *he's* the one being oppressed, have an open discussion of privilege and what other people go through. This can be hard for young people to understand, so use personal examples of friends and family to help him see. You can also do this by watching a movie or reading a book together.

If your son is "just asking questions" about difficult subjects, like the Holocaust or the US Civil War, don't shy away from them! Instead, join him in his investigations. Read, listen, and watch a lot of sources, from published textbooks to expert accounts to eyewitness testimony. If he says that you can't trust mainstream accounts, ask him why and where he heard that. Promote curiosity without leaning into total skepticism!

In the case of a young man who's feeling spiritually or communally lost, help him find his way. Help him join groups, try different things out, and reach out to others who feel the same. Participate along with him to check in on these groups and to show him that he's not alone in feeling lost. If your son insists that it's only the old, discriminatory traditions that he can find meaning in, ask him about the people they leave behind—people who are excluded because of their gender, sex, or race. Again, many young people have a hard time empathizing with these things, so be sure to use personal examples from his life, his community, or media!

If your son is already in the grips of the right-wing, you'll have to remain empathetic with him as a parent while also keeping distance. Your goal will be to show him that you don't approve of his behavior or his beliefs without disapproving so hard that it only drives him further away from you, to the point that he can only find community among others on the right. I am not going to sugar coat this. Threading this needle will be incredibly hard.

In all likelihood, you'll be able to use many of the same techniques and conversation guides provided elsewhere in this book. Just because your son is a self-avowed member of the right-wing *now* doesn't mean that he'll be that way forever, or that this is an inherent or core part of him. This might indeed be a phase! Whether it is or not, you'll want to show empathy and care without accepting or condoning his beliefs.

But one important thing has changed—your son has crossed a line by becoming active in right-wing circles. This means that you'll need to establish some boundaries. First, you'll need to separate yourself from contributing to right-wing activities, such as withdrawing financial support, not giving rides, or restricting access to computers or other online devices. Second, you'll need to tell him that if he continues down this path, he will be jeopardizing your relationship with him. You will need to word this carefully so that it's not a threat, but a statement of fact. You just refuse to be personally involved with people who are fascists. And finally, you'll need to prepare yourself to take more drastic action if it turns out that your son is involved in violent activities.

Most people who are interested in fascism, or who have come to identify with fascism or a fascist movement, aren't immediately at risk of engaging in physical violence. They will certainly engage in verbal and social violence, but that doesn't mean that you need to jump straight to calling the police. Instead, think of him as not being lost yet, but being on the path to being recruited. He's in danger, but you can help get him out of it.

I spoke with Gina Longan, Director of NCITE, a think tank operating out of the University of Nebraska, Omaha, that focuses on researching and understanding radicalization pathways in the United States. Much of their recent work focuses on these paths of recruitment and how parents and others in the lives of the young men who join extremist organizations experience barriers to preventing their joining.

"It's just heartbreaking to talk to these families," Gina said, "[T]hey just feel so guilty, they feel like they didn't know . . . they feel like they saw what their sons were getting into but they didn't do anything." This guilt made it harder for these parents to reach out to their peers about keeping their kids out of the right-wing, but it also made it harder for them to seek help from outside sources.

I talked with Erin Kearns at NCITE, who works on referral pathways for teens and youth who are on the road to committing extremist violence. Her research and policy work involves parents, teachers, kids, and law enforcement, all of whom are having to get more and more serious about what to do if a kid seems like they're headed in the direction of white supremacist violence and organizing. She's most interested in what happens when things go really wrong—when a kid moves all the way from an interest in violence to making a plan to commit violence themselves.

Erin says that "40% of adults don't know" what they're supposed to do when they notice extremist or mass violent tendencies in a kid—they might've heard the "see something, say something" messaging from law enforcement but don't know what that something is or to whom they're supposed to say something. She says that the work of educators and researchers like her is to help people "take steps back and at the most basic level identify the concerning little pieces of behavior," the things that come long before a kid "looks up how to build a bomb."

"Most people don't notice the parts that come earlier on that evolutionary path toward radical violence," she says. And even if they do see signs that concern them and wonder what they should do about it, "they're worried, and don't want to get people in trouble, don't want to report people." She says that this comes from a misunderstanding of how the formal pathways for reporting potentially violent activity work, and that means that all too often warning signs go unnoticed and ignored. "The fear of getting people in trouble is why we see people who know there's a potential threat way before there's weapon acquisition."

If your son has reached this point—where he is involved in groups that are violent or are planning violence, or he is in a community that has encouraged him to do so himself—then things have escalated to the point that what he is doing could be called "terrorism." Most security experts and scholars define terrorism as the use of force or threats of force by any non-state political group to achieve a desired goal. This means that if your son is, say, a member of the Proud Boys and they are marching in the street to try to stop a drag show from being held in a public park, he is engaging in terrorism.

Terrorist activity comes in many varieties and comes with its own set of laws and procedures that differ by country. In some jurisdictions, it is illegal to share content like hate speech or misinformation, let alone to act on it. In some cases, you might be liable for some consequences if you are aware of plans or motives held by your son but do nothing about it. If you are worried about your son to the extent that you are considering contacting law enforcement, know that you aren't alone. Other parents have gone through the same set of decisions and thoughts, and others have dealt with the same feelings you might be having now. There are also many organizations that can help you—and your son—through that process. It might also help you to know that most of the time when law enforcement gets reports about young men who are suspected of violence or violent intentions, it's their parents who have done the reporting.

"If it's gotten to the point that you're concerned about their safety or the safety of others," Erin says, "Most school districts have something called a behavioral team, or a threat assessment team, to assess what's going on with potential threats." This group of people includes administrators, law enforcement, and sometimes researchers and other experts. These teams are the place to go whether or not the threat involves a school. "The team will hear about any reported threat and decide if it's an imminent threat," that is, if the possibility of violence is real and could happen soon, "and if that's the case then it'll go to law enforcement or possibly to the FBI," if things are serious enough. "One of the benefits of these teams," Erin says, "is that oftentimes what the kids are doing isn't a criminal act, so law enforcement can't be involved except in an advisory capacity—they're not gonna lock anybody up for most of this."

I can't claim to know what it feels like to be worried about your son committing violent acts in the name of the right. If you are in that situation, know that you have my sympathy. Obviously, I won't try to tell you that reporting your son to the police or other law enforcement is likely to help your relationship with him. But if you are worried about your son committing an act of violence, however small, know that everyone else in your community is counting on you to do what you can to stop him.

That's what happens when things go wrong, when kids fall through the cracks and don't get the help or intervention they need to be steered away from violence. But when this system works right, it's the best way we currently have to prevent kids from engaging in major violence.

The following is a list of law enforcement resources that you can reach out to in the case that you are concerned about potential violent activity from your son.

- First, if you're dealing with a young man who's still in school, reach out through his school first. It's possible that the school already has a system in place for referring young men who are at risk of engaging in extremist violence.
- If you are in the United States or the United Kingdom, there are several organizations you might reach out to if your school district doesn't have such a task force, or if you're dealing with a young man who is no longer in school. Some local jurisdictions have their own counterterrorism forces, primarily in major cities:
  - NYC, the Office of Counter Terrorism: 1–866-SAFENYS
  - LA, via the LAPD: 1–877-A-THREAT
- Depending on where you live, there are national-level options for you to reach out to. These include:
  - FBI: 1-310-477-6565
  - UK Home Office: 0800 789 321
  - If there is an immediate emergency, you can call your local police department

- If you live outside the United States or United Kingdom, look into your national police office or other law enforcement.

Please proceed with caution when contacting law enforcement about your son or about anyone. It may be your only option if you are concerned that your son is planning a dangerous act, but it will expose him to lethal danger from the police and other law enforcement officials. Use these options as a last resort.

I expect to get some flak from some on the left for suggesting that you might want to contact law enforcement at all when it comes to someone's potential fascist activity. There are many progressives and left-wing believers who would argue that involving law enforcement will only cause more violence or further empower the state. The fact is that I don't disagree with these perspectives. But I would argue that in the case of extremist right-wing violence, we need to sometimes take an approach of harm reduction—trying to stop violence from spreading or expanding.

This chapter has been a succinct guide to how to talk to your son about fascism, but by itself, it isn't enough. Here is a list of other resources you might use or take a look at in your ongoing conversations with your son.

- The American Civil Liberties Union, the Southern Poverty Law Center, and the Anti-Defamation League all maintain helpful databases on fascist and other far-right groups in the United States.
- The group "Antifascist Europe" maintains a database of far-right groups in Europe.
- Check out the organizations of people I've quoted in this book! CIVIX and Moonshot are both great places to look for guidance on engaging with radicalized youth.
- Check in with educators, psychologists, and other parenting experts for general guidance on how to talk to children and young adults about tough subjects. A lot of that advice is helpful here too!

Notes

1 A good place to start would be the works of Shane Burley, or Bray, Mark, *Antifa: The Anti-Fascist Handbook*. Brooklyn, NY: Melville House Publishing, 2017.
2 There's been extensive reporting about this issue, and Musk's indifference (or outright hostility) toward the monitoring of harassment and extremism on Twitter/X. Even a cursory Google search about this issue will yield hundreds of news stories covering his elimination of the site's previous content moderation teams, as well as the resignation of the leader of their Trust and Safety team.

5

WOMEN AND NONBINARY CHILDREN

As I said in Chapter 2, fascists disproportionately target young men for recruitment. That's both because of the specific social and political problems facing young men and also because fascist politics tend toward the benefit of young men in particular—a chicken-and-egg situation. But this doesn't mean that there are no young women who become interested in fascism or that fascism doesn't appeal to women.

Historically, there have always been female fascists alongside their male counterparts. Fascist groups like the Nazis and the Italian Fascists had female auxiliaries for both adult and young women. The female counterpart to the Hitler Youth, the League of German Girls, was compulsory for young women from ages 10 to 18. Adult women were able to join the Nazi Party, though they were admitted on a more selective basis than men and only numbered about 5% of the party membership by the time the Nazis took power.

Young women have continued their involvement in fascist and far-right-wing movements since the defeat of the big fascist movements in the early 20th century. They joined post-fascist parties in Spain and Austria, they joined skinhead groups in the 1990s, and they participate in the alt-right today.

Fascism and Young Women

Fascism appeals to some young women for the same reasons it appeals to some young men. Young women are just as capable as young men of being drawn into racist thinking or of thinking that strong, dictatorial leadership is the right thing for their community or country. Some are drawn in by their peers or relatives, and others join more or less because it's what their friend group is doing, and they don't want to be left out.

DOI: 10.4324/9781003385509-6

Some women are simply true believers in fascism. The first openly fascist organization in British history was founded by a woman, Rotha Beryl Lintorn Orman.[1] She had a military family background and was among a group of young women who showed up at an early Scouts meeting (this was the movement that would later evolve into the Boy Scouts)—her and her friends' presence would inspire the creation of the Girl Guides. She then volunteered during WWI as a hospital worker.

Fascism was new and exciting, and Lintorn Orman was caught up in that excitement. She was motivated to found the British Fascisti (later renamed the British Fascists) in 1923 by the successful anti-communist purges of the Italian Fascist Party. Like many elites of the time, she admired the Italian Fascists for their violence and perceived vitality and hoped that she might be able to reproduce that kind of fervor in the United Kingdom. Her gender was held against her, however, as was her promiscuous personal life, and her organization was sidelined after a few years with the foundation of the British Union of Fascists by male politician Oswald Mosley. Lintorn Orman's life ended early, before WWII. Her party splintered, and she descended into alcohol and drug abuse. She died in 1935 at 40.

Lintorn Orman's story illustrates how some people turn to fascism because it's the fashion of the time. Fascism provided useful language and symbols for her existing hatred of the left and minorities and garnered her press and word-of-mouth support for her new movement. This opportunistic fascism can capture both men and women and is something we see clearly today, too.

Many women join fascist movements for the same reason men do—because they earnestly believe in the promise of fascism. One example is Beate Zschäpe, a German neo-Nazi and member of the National Socialist Underground. Zschäpe, who was born in East Germany behind the Iron Curtain, spent several years as one of the ringleaders of a mass-murderous fascist terrorist organization that killed 15 people during a several-year campaign. She remains imprisoned for her crimes.

Other women join with fascists because of the legacy it holds for their country or their community. One example is Giorgia Meloni, who became the Prime Minister of Italy in 2023. Meloni was born in working-class Rome and joined the Italian Social Movement party as a young woman. The Italian Social Movement was the party that grew out of the then-banned Italian Fascist Party in 1946, making it the closest thing to fascism that was legal in Italy at the time. Meloni seems to earnestly believe in the examples of fascism for herself and for her country. She is on record admiring Mussolini for his resolve and saying that Adolf Hitler was a "complex figure" who can't be judged too easily.

Meloni emphasizes her femininity and motherhood when she discusses politics, talking about the need to give birth to a new nation and the men and women who must sacrifice to make that happen. She also uses her traditional feminine roles to justify her opposition to queerness and non-normative femininity, including her calls to end access to abortions. Meloni is part of a new wave of female leaders of the far right that stretches from Alice Weidel[2] in Germany to Marjorie Taylor Greene in the United States. These women embody both the fiery anger present in masculine right-wing personalities while insisting that their being women gives them caring, concerned insights into the lives and needs of children—a talking point they use to oppose queer rights.

Women are also everyday foot soldiers in right-wing movements. Getting much less press than their female leader counterparts, these women generally operate in the background of contemporary fascist and right-wing movements, or specifically work on recruitment.

The neo-Nazi skinhead movement of the 1990s had many women in it, among them Shannon Martinez, who has given many interviews throughout her life regarding her experiences in the white power movement. In interviews given later in life, after she'd left the movement, she said that she joined in order to have a stable community while she was moving around the country in her teenage years.

She was also drawn to the violence and intensity of the movement, like many of the people who joined it. Skinheads in the 1990s were the new, radical, exciting wing of the fascist world—they were young, they were angry, and they were active. She recounts how she and her fellow fascists "threw tear gas into a gay club," "attacked people's homes" with BB guns and "attended Klu Klux Klan rallies."[3]

In interviews, Martinez says that she didn't initially join up because of racism— at first, it was a way to "displace" her feelings of not belonging to other people. She felt socially isolated and excluded from the world and needed it to be someone else's fault. She sought belonging among some of her peers and an explanation for why she didn't belong in other contexts. In some ways, the skinheads were just like any other subculture, giving her a place to be herself and to belong to a peer group. But more than other subcultures, they gave supposed explanations for why she felt so alone and isolated. It was the Jews and Black people who controlled the system, the erosion of white culture, and the loss of racial purity. This kept her and her fellow skinheads from having to confront their own role in the oppression of others or from thinking about systemic reasons that the world works the way it does.

Once inside the movement, women in far-right organizations often note the movement's abusiveness and the degree of control that the men tried to hold over them. Martinez and others spoke of being harassed by male members of the movement or of being directly abused by their partners—who, by social pressure, had to be already established members of the same right-wing movement, further isolating them from the rest of the world.

The romantic and sexual connections were a central part of getting women involved in skinhead culture. Researchers note that many women who joined the movement did so because their boyfriends joined, and that these abusive men then required their partners to follow them.[4] Other women were recruited explicitly because the men in the movement knew that they would encourage more men to join.

Once in the movement, skinhead women faced a difficult tightrope. Violence and power were rewarded in the skinhead world, but as women, they were expected to be submissive and accepting of the power that the men in the group had over them.

Their dress was also heavily policed. Too mainstream, and they could be punished for looking like they were trying to leave the group, but dressing too much like other skinheads would make them look masculine and unattractive, unlike the feminine ideal they were being held up to.

Martinez says that she got out of the skinhead movement when one of her neo-Nazi boyfriends' mothers took her into her confidence. She helped her get a job outside the movement, which meant that she started talking to people outside it. For the first time in years, she was getting perspectives from people who weren't white nationalists and whose identities weren't rooted in fascism. Instead, she was talking to people who had everyday concerns about their families and loved ones. That was enough for Martinez to start breaking out of her fascist echo chamber.

Today, Martinez works on helping other young women out of fascist movements. She focuses on the emotional and belonging piece rather than the ideological ones. She says that when she was a neo-Nazi, it was because she wanted to belong to something bigger than herself.

These examples show many of the reasons that young women might join a fascist movement, which are broadly similar to the reasons that it might appeal to young men or anyone. Some people are just true believers in what fascism has to say, while others are persuadable due to their social or cultural position. And if a young person grows up in a time that is just more susceptible to fascist growth, such as the one we're in now, there's an even greater chance that they'll end up interested in or affiliated with fascism or the far right.

But what about the inherent misogyny of fascism? Wouldn't that keep women away from it? The issue is complicated, but the simple one is "no." Many people believe things that are contrary to their own material interests—consider a union worker who votes for politicians who advocate for free trade and outsourcing or a high-income voter who chooses a candidate who will raise their taxes. These people make their political decisions out of real conviction, not just by calculating which policy will directly benefit them the most.

Many women earnestly believe they are subordinate to men or inferior to them in ways that should keep them out of power. These women are very susceptible to right-wing messaging and ideology since they've already bought what fascism is selling. While the misogyny of fascism and the far right does reduce the ability of fascists to recruit young women, it doesn't eliminate it altogether. This means that even if your child is a girl, you'll still need to watch for right-wing sentiment and fascist leanings in her and her friends.

A contemporary example of a women-oriented movement in fascism is known as "tradwife." A portmanteau of "traditional wives," the "tradwife" scene is characterized by sharing images of women in 1950s or late 1800s-style clothing who are cooking, cleaning, or caring for children in what most people assume are traditional ways. The women in these images are as beautiful as supermodels and revel in their submission to their husbands and their social roles as caregivers and bearers of children. Many of the people who pitch this content are, in fact, not stay-at-home parents but professional influencers, but that doesn't stop their content from advocating what they call a "return" to social norms from previous decades.[5] Whether or not these women actually practice what they preach, their influence is widespread and is exactly the kind of thing you should check to make sure isn't taking over your daughter's social media feeds.

Trans and Nonbinary People

As gender norms shift and more and more gender identities are recognized and expressed, there are more young people who come out as gender non-conforming, gender neutral, and transgender. As you might suspect, these young people's identities and behaviors often make them targets for harassment, oppression, and violence from the right-wing—but that doesn't stop some of them from becoming right-wing themselves.

By the mid-2020s, the idea that there might be trans neo-Nazis may seem impossible. Fascists and the far-right throughout the world have landed on an extreme anti-queer position in the last few years, using anti-trans ideology as the center of their politics—or at least as its most basic entry point for potential recruits and fellow travelers. They've made the idea of "grooming" a mainstream concept. "Grooming" is a right-wing conspiracy theory based on the assumption that queer people are pedophiles and that they use their nonconforming gender and sexuality to recruit young people to be gay or trans. This conspiracy theory is the basis for the right-wing's push to oppose queer education in schools or to eliminate all references to sex in education.

But the fact is that there are, and have been, trans people and other gender nonconforming people who have embraced far-right-wing ideologies.

One example is Jessica Marie Watkins. She founded a branch of the Oath Keepers, a group of US military veterans who embrace militia ideologies. Before transitioning, Watkins served in the US Army in Afghanistan. After she transitioned, she was dismissed from the military, changed her name, and started a small right-wing militia in Ohio after being disavowed by her family. As the leader of a militia, she organized demonstrations and armed drills to prepare her militia for what she believed was a coming confrontation between the forces of order and those of disorder.

She got her wish in the form of the January 6 attempted coup of President Donald Trump. Watkins led her militia to the Capitol building to work with the Oath Keepers and invaded Congress wearing tactical gear. She was the only Oath Keeper leader to be acquitted on charges of seditious conspiracy but was sentenced on one count of conspiracy to obstruct an official proceeding—namely counting the Electoral College votes that would elect Joe Biden. She was sentenced to eight and a half years in prison.[6] Though she's since disavowed Trump and the Oath Keepers, Watkins maintains that her arrest and imprisonment were orchestrated by the same kind of outside forces that she argued had made the insurrection necessary in the first place.

Watkins's example shows us that even people whom we would assume would stay as far away from the right-wing as possible are sometimes caught up in it. While you have much, much less to worry about when it comes to the possibility of a nonbinary child getting interested in the far right, you should still keep an eye on any conspiratorial thinking they might end up holding in their heads.

Exceptions aside, fascism and the far right have distanced themselves from nonbinary and trans people, especially among the young. If you are a caretaker for a trans or nonbinary youth, it's far more likely that you'll be dealing with fascism and the right-wing as a threat to your child than as a danger they might fall into themselves.

How to Talk to a Young Woman or Nonbinary Child About Fascism

Talking about fascism with your daughter, nonbinary child, or trans child will be very different from talking about it with your son, but there are some factors that will be almost exactly the same. Namely, the core advice I'd like to give you is to listen to your child with empathy. You should approach this conversation with curiosity, calm, and care, knowing that there will be many factors in your child's life that you're unaware of and opinions they may have that could surprise you.

It *is* possible that when you speak to your daughter about the dangers of misogyny and the right-wing, she will express right-wing or gender discriminatory views of her own. While this might be more surprising than encountering these viewpoints in a young man, it can't be a complete surprise—there have been many young and adult women throughout history who have shared right-wing politics with their male counterparts. With the current and ongoing rise of right-wing politics in youth culture, this should unfortunately come as no surprise.

Still, talking to your daughter or gender nonconforming child about fascism will probably be a warning conversation rather than an informative or exploratory one. This will likely parallel the conversations that I've compared the "fascism talk" to, namely talking to your child about sex. For young men, this is generally a conversation about how to behave ethically, while for young women it is a conversation about potential dangers and what can be done to avoid or overcome them.

Start by asking your child what they've heard that relates to the right-wing. In the case of young women, pay special attention to what they say that relates to misogyny, and with trans or nonbinary children, pay attention to what they've heard about trans identity or "grooming." Ideally, you've already had a conversation with your child about gender discrimination, misogyny, and gender bias, but if you haven't, now is always a good time to start! Many young girls start to experience sexual and gender discrimination at or even before the age of 12, much younger than many people have the conversations we're talking about.[7]

When you ask your child about their experiences, listen. Listen closely—they may surprise you! Your daughter might claim that she's never experienced the kind of gender or sex discrimination you're discussing, or she might turn out to have a fully formed feminism. In either case, remember that your role is transitioning from leader and teacher to colleague and advisor as your child ages. Whether they are 10 or 25, they're increasingly too old to be told by you what's right and what's wrong.

If your child already shows an understanding of the right-wing's danger to them, you'll have an easier start. It's possible you'll start this conversation and your child will already be on board about the dangers of misogyny and sexism and how they connect to threats to other marginalized people. If that's the case, great! You can skip right to some of the conversation strategies I talk about in Chapter 6, on how we can fight fascism together.

One way to get a conversation going would be to bring up a popular right-wing influencer. In 2023, that would be Andrew Tate, but if you're reading this in several years, the relevant name is likely to have changed. Do some research and read some news articles before you have this conversation. Ask your child if they've heard of this person or if they've heard their classmates or friends discussing them. The conversation will be different depending on if your child's friends are mostly other women, trans, or nonbinary children, or boys.

Ask your child if they've ever seen or heard any of this person's content and what they think about it. Listen to them, and after that, share your perspective. Talk about how that rhetoric makes you feel and what kind of danger it poses. Share some of the things you've learned in this book and elsewhere about how the right-wing uses gender and sex politics to attack and harm people. Make it clear that you're an ally of theirs.

Just like a conversation with a son, this part will depend heavily on your own gender. If you are a woman, you could share how hearing the things that people like Tate say about women makes you feel—it might make you angry or uncomfortable, or it might be threatening. Share and explain your feelings with your child, and then tell them where they're coming from. Whether your child acknowledges it or not, you do have more perspective on life than she does. Now is the time to share those experiences. You can use those personal stories and combine them with the history that's in Chapter 1 of this book to talk to your daughter about how somebody like Tate—who might seem innocuous, just an internet personality—can move and shake the world.

If you are a man and are talking to your child about how the right-wing, gender, and sexual violence are connected, you'll have to talk from a different starting point. It'll be less likely that you can share examples of sex discrimination that you've experienced, and even if you have, I would suggest leaving them out of this conversation. Instead, double down on listening and hearing your child out. You're inviting them to share vulnerable, uncomfortable things with you that both of you know you can't fully comprehend because of your own gender. Ask your child if they've experienced discrimination based on their gender, and what that looked or felt like. Ask them if they've seen something like that happen to their friends or fellow students. And ask them how the boys or young men around them talk about gender.

What your child says might surprise you, or even frighten you. They might talk about gender and sexual violence they or other people around them have experienced. Or they might be quiet and not want to talk to you about it at all. As the parent or caretaker of an adolescent or teenager, I'm sure you're familiar with that. If your child doesn't want to talk to you about it, one option would be to find someone they feel more comfortable talking to—a relative or trusted friend, or a therapist or counselor.

No matter your gender, this is a conversation where you need to acknowledge that your child is entering a phase of life where you can't protect them from the negative experiences they're likely to encounter. This is a terrible, terrible thing to have to think about, and possibly worse to tell your child, but it's important to be honest about. You're reading this book because you know that the right-wing poses a danger to your child and to the whole world, and they're of an age when they'll have to face that head-on.

Fascism and Safety

When it comes to fascism, your priority with your female or nonbinary child should be their personal safety and the safety of their community. That means you'll need to help them keep an eye on their friends and what's happening at their school.

If your daughter or nonbinary child tells you that they've been hearing or seeing right-wing content at school or elsewhere, you'll need to make an evaluation for yourself. One possibility is that you understand that, unfortunately, these threats are a part of the world that your child lives in. Another approach is to escalate the situation and see these threats as real challenges to your child's safety. If you choose to escalate the situation, you'll need to be prepared for the world around you to undermine you or your concerns. The public world has a real interest in denying the dangers of fascism, and especially in justifying the comments and threats that it results in by saying that "boys will be boys."

Please don't accept this explanation or excuse. Instead, demand that your child be able to live and grow in safety. This is especially important if your child is nonbinary, as fascists and the far right target people who are trans or otherwise gender nonconforming for outsized physical and verbal violence.

If your young daughter does fall into fascism or gets interested in the right-wing, you should approach the issue with the same kind of sympathy and care that you would with your son. Understand that when dealing with children—or anyone—who has fallen in with the right-wing, you are dealing with two issues. On the surface is the ideological, where they might use fascist talking points or start to apply fascist thinking in their everyday lives. They might use swears or slurs they would never have considered otherwise, or they might start to redirect their lives based on what their ideology tells them.

But that's just the surface. Underneath that is likely a young person who feels isolated for some reason. They might have lost friends or loved ones, or they might be finding it hard to make friends in a new place. They might have a mental or emotional condition that makes it difficult to connect with others. Seeking membership in a group of people who are also on the outskirts of society can be a good way for a teenager or young person to find their way socially. In some ways, it's even better if that group is so ostracized that joining it only isolates them *further* from the rest of the world—that means the people in the group are less likely to leave!

This means that if you're talking to a teenager or young person who's gotten involved in a subculture like this, your first move shouldn't be to try to argue with her about the merits of her thinking. You can't start by talking about how fascism and the right-wing are misogynist, or how they could be the victims of the oppression they're advocating. That's a public-facing argument, the sort of thing that belongs in a televised debate. Around the kitchen table or in the minivan, you're not debating the merits of fascist ideology. You're talking about feelings and belonging.

It's much more likely, though, that your daughter, trans, or nonbinary child will be facing danger from fascists and right-wing sources rather than joining one. If that's the case, be sure that you show up to be an ally and protector in their corner. While they are increasingly adults as they enter middle and high school, and are fully adults when college-aged, young people still need your support and protection.

If your child is encountering bullying for their gender or sex, it's your job to help them. This might mean confronting their school bureaucracy, or confronting other parents. It might mean losing family members or friends. I ask that you remember that your child needs you, your support, and your love, especially if their life is made more difficult by being a member of a marginalized or oppressed group.

Chapter 6 will give you more advice on how to stand up against fascism and the far right-wing in your community. The most important advice I have is to be sure that your child knows you're with them, and then to act on that promise by sticking up for them when they're confronted by sexism, misogyny, anti-queer politics, or whatever it is that might be hurting them. Take their concerns seriously, and help them develop the tools they need to keep themselves safe.

Fascism in the Family

In the case that you have one or more sons who are interested in fascism or who are engaging in right-wing politics, you have an additional responsibility alongside trying to help them out of it—you'll need to help protect any other children you have from them. This isn't to say that a fascist sibling is more likely to be violent against their sister or nonbinary sibling, but rather that it's likely they will make comments and judgments that would be damaging to them.[8]

In this case, you'll have to carefully balance caretaking for each of your children by protecting your other child from damaging abuse while trying to maintain the empathy and concern necessary to keep a right-leaning son from becoming so alienated from you and his family that he will sink further into the right-wing.

One way that a male sibling who is getting involved with the right-wing might hurt or seek to abuse his sister or nonbinary sibling is by indirect sexual abuse. This can happen via online or in-person "slut-shaming," something that happens when someone uses the real or assumed sexual activity of a woman against her in order to make people think less of her. "Slut shamers" insult people for being sexually active or for having more sexual partners than is socially acceptable. It can also happen whether a person is sexually active or not, simply because they're a woman, or because they use makeup, or because of how they're dressed.

Men on the right-wing regularly use this tactic against women in order to exert power over them, hoping that internalized shame will stop them from pursuing their romantic or sexual interests. They might also be hoping that the rest of society will jump on the same bandwagon. These tactics and perspectives were important in the "GamerGate" online abuse community, when hundreds to thousands of men spent years harassing women and nonbinary people in the video game industry for their looks, their sexual activities, and their gender.

If your son is far into the right-wing, it's possible he'll engage in directly harmful behavior. He may make insulting comments or posts about his siblings to right-wing friends in person or online, and may even share non-consensual photos of his siblings with his peers. This is not only deeply unethical; it is also illegal in many jurisdictions in the United States and elsewhere.

Through all this, you'll need to prioritize the safety of your most vulnerable child. If your son is being violent, physically or verbally, he'll need to know that that is a red line. No amount of empathy for your son should let you threaten the safety or privacy of your other children.

If your son engages in this kind of behavior, it's time to take some drastic measures. I have to counsel you against treating these or other similar activities as typical sibling rivalry. These acts cross the line into the dangerous and even the criminal. That means that if you find your son sharing pictures of your other children or their friends online, or harassing them in a gendered way, you need to know that not only is he liable for potential criminal prosecution—you yourself are potentially at legal risk. And while this book so far has encouraged you to have sympathy for your son even if he is exploring fascist ideology, I encourage you to shelve that feeling if he is actively harming one of your other children. After you've done the work protecting your other children, then you can try to salvage something with your son.

Now that you have some skills and tactics to talk with your daughters or nonbinary children about fascism, we're ready for the last chapter in this book—it'll help you and your family learn to fight fascism together. Chapter 6 has suggestions for how you can stop the spread of fascism in your community and country.

Notes

1 Cullen, Stephen, "Four Women for Mosley: Women in the British Union of Fascists, 1932–1940," *Oral History* 24, no. 1 (1996): 49–59. www.jstor.org/stable/40179498.
2 Weidel is a lesbian and the leader of the *Alternative für Deutschland*, in English "Alternative for Germany" or AfD. Her own gender and sexuality do not prevent her from advocating against homosexual marriage and the influence of so-called "gender ideology."
3 Rihl, Juliette, "What to Do if Your Loved One Is a White Supremacist or in Danger of Radicalization," January 26, 2021. www.publicsource.com.
4 Valeri, Robin Maria, and Borgeson, Kevin, *Skinhead History, Identity, and Culture.* New York: Routledge, 2018.
5 Grose, Jessica, "'Tradwife' Content Isn't Really for Women," *New York Times*, May 15, 2024.
6 Riley, Ryan J., Barnes, Daniel, and Glisson, Fiona, "Self-Proclaimed 'Idiot' Oath Keeper Sentenced to More Than 8 Years in January 6 Case," *NBC News*, May 26, 2023.
7 See the Rainn Institute for more information on this www.rainn.org/statistics/victims-sexual-violence.
8 There's even evidence to suggest that young men with sisters are more likely to become conservative: Healy, Andrew, and Malhotra, Neil, "Childhood Socialization and Political Attitudes: Evidence from a Natural Experiment," *The Journal of Politics* 75, no. 4 (2013): 1023–37. https://doi.org/10.1017/s0022381613000996.

6

FIGHTING FASCISM TOGETHER

Now that you've had the important conversations with your son about fascism and the right-wing that we discussed in the previous chapters, it's time to work with him as an ally and a friend in the fight against fascism. This doesn't mean that your role as a parent and mentor is over—instead, it means that you're transitioning to being more like equals in the fight against the rise of the extreme right-wing. You'll still need to be there to guide him in the right direction, and you'll still need to be his support and sounding board for when he encounters something he's not prepared for or doesn't know the answer to.

You'll also learn how to fight against the rise of fascism in your community and your country. One of the most tried-and-true ways of fighting fascism is by confronting it wherever it appears. This is how countries like the United Kingdom, France, and the United States avoided having big and successful fascist organizations like those in Germany and Italy. People stepped up, protested against fascists, organized against them, and made sure their propaganda didn't go unanswered. This chapter will give you some suggestions and resources you can access to figure out how to join protests against fascism wherever you live.

Fighting fascism together means building a family that stands up to fascism and the extreme right-wing whenever and wherever you encounter it. It means giving up on being a bystander, or saying that politics just isn't "your thing" or that it's not an appropriate topic of conversation. This genie can't go back in the bottle. If you want to be serious about fighting fascism, it has to be part of your life.

History of Antifascism

"Antifa" has gotten a lot of bad press in the United States and the Western world recently. It's been blamed for property destruction, the spread of urban anarchy,

DOI: 10.4324/9781003385509-7

"woke culture," and, bizarrely, even for Donald Trump's attempted coup on January 6, 2021. Most of the time commentators talk about Antifa as if it were a dedicated, cohesive group, some kind of national committee like the Republican Party or a centralized terrorist organization like Al-Qaeda. They accuse "Antifa" of being a violent movement to overthrow the government.

These are all myths—in fact, they're right-wing propaganda. "Antifa" is just a shortened form of "antifascist," a widespread, disorganized movement that's better compared to "feminists" or "libertarians" than it is to a centralized political body. Antifascists come in all kinds of political stripes, from anarchists who do in fact want to eventually overthrow the government, to socialists and liberal democrats who want to reform the government, to conservatives who just don't want fascists taking over their country. If you're reading this book because you don't want your son to be a fascist, congratulations! You're a part of antifa.

Antifascists are as old as fascism itself, if not older—people were opposing the power of violent right-wing groups years before they started calling themselves fascists. From the first days of Mussolini's Fascist Party, people organized to try to stop him from propaganda and taking power. They marched against the Fascists' coup, fought them in the streets, and organized underground to limit their reach. Many of them were injured, imprisoned, or even killed for their trouble. Today, these people are rightly regarded as heroes by many—except by fascists, of course.

In countries where fascists never fully took over, it's antifa we have to thank. Antifascist demonstrators did a lot of work to keep Oswald Mosley's British Union of Fascists from gaining popularity among working-class Englishmen in the 1930s. Antifascist organizers like WEB Du Bois and the members of the Communist Party worked against the rise of the Silver Shirts in the United States. And, of course, every soldier and worker who contributed to the war effort against the Nazis was fighting the rise of fascism. All of these men and women were antifascists, and I am grateful to them for their sacrifices in the name of keeping the world safe from the dangers of the extreme right-wing.

During and after WWII, the two biggest opponents of Germany, the United States and the USSR, leaned heavily into antifascist propaganda. Both countries emphasized the dangers and barbarity of fascism, in Germany especially. This messaging was everywhere and at all levels of popular consumption. There were antifascist movies, antifascist comics, antifascist posters, and antifascist songs. One short film called "Don't Be a Sucker," produced by the US War Department (precursor to the contemporary Department of Defense) in 1947, warned against the potential that the very same fascist ideology the United States had just defeated could get a foothold at home. The film features Academy Award-winning actors warning against racism, discrimination, and bigotry. Even Dr. Seuss, famed children's author and illustrator, was heavily involved in the effort to produce antifascist messaging in the United States. Back then, people understood that fascism meant an end to democracy and the rise of racism.

After WWII, fascism was a lot less powerful, but that didn't mean that antifascists let their guards down. They hunted down Nazis who had escaped prosecution and submitted them to authorities in Europe so that they could stand trial. They identified people who profited off of their collaboration with the Nazis and the Italian Fascists and tried to get them labeled forever as outcasts for having worked with the Nazis. By the 1960s and 70s, when fascist organizing had returned to the Western world in earnest, antifascists worked in their communities and subcultures to keep them free of fascists. One example is the SHARPS, Skinheads Against Racial Prejudice, who try to keep alive the multicultural celebration that was skinhead culture in the 1960s, before it was co-opted by right-wing and white supremacist thinking.[1] Another example is Anti-Racist Action, a network of anarchists and other leftists who work to prevent the rise of fascism in their communities and on the national and international level.

This work continues in the present day. Today, antifascists do all kinds of work to try to stop the rise of the extreme right-wing. Some are academics, studying fascism and how it's developed over time. Some are legislators and lawyers, trying to see fascists answer for their crimes. Some are public figures, trying to keep people from seeing fascist messaging unanswered in the public sphere. Some are demonstrators, making sure that fascists can't occupy public space without answering to their opponents.

One antifascist group that's often overlooked might surprise you—conservatives. Mainstream right-wing politicians and political groups are some of the most opposed to fascism as a whole and often join up with centrists and leftists to fight fascism. They also fight fascism on their own, keeping it out of their meetings and movements, and policing their youth to make sure they don't fall down the rabbit hole. For a contemporary example, you can think of the "never Trump" Republicans in the United States, who don't want Trump and his coalition to take over their party more than they already have. Historical examples would be French conservatives like Charles de Gaulle's opposition to the Nazi takeover of his country. The fact is that conservatives also oppose the kind of right-wing revolution that fascists want. This is why I wrote at the beginning of this book that you don't need to be progressive to be an antifascist. All you need is to want to stop fascists from taking power.

The history of antifascist work fills many other books. See this note for some examples.[2] But that's not what this book is for. Instead, I'm going to spend the rest of this chapter showing you ways that you and your son can be part of this effort to keep fascism out of your community.

Fighting Fascism in Public

In Chapter 4 of this book, I talked about the difference between fighting fascism in private and fighting it in public. I've spent this entire book so far talking about how to fight fascism in private, by keeping your son out of fascist circles. In this private world, empathy is your best weapon against fascism. It's how you can maintain a connection with your son without losing your moral ground when it comes to the extreme right-wing.

This chapter is different. Instead of talking about fighting fascism in your home, we'll be talking about how to stop it from growing in your community—what some academics call the "public sphere."

The public sphere is a very different place from the private one. In public, we assume that you don't know the people you're dealing with. They might be strangers, or at most loose acquaintances. Since you don't know them, you can't assume that they have your interests at heart, or that they care about what you have to say or how you feel. And you can't assume that they have any interest in keeping you safe or in hearing you out.

You are in a much more vulnerable spot without that safety. Fighting fascism in public can be more dangerous than it was in private since, as I mentioned in Chapter 1, fascists are organized specifically to fight for control of the public sphere. If you know them personally, you can try to short-circuit their hatred, but if you don't, you won't make any headway by appealing to their heart. Instead, you'll have to meet them on the same ground they're fighting on—the control of public spaces.

Some of the tactics discussed in previous chapters might be useful when confronting fascists in public. Many people find it helpful to remember that those they oppose are someone else's son, someone else's father, or friend. Using that empathy can be vital in working with people and groups that are only close to the right-wing but which haven't fallen too far to be rescued. You might find yourself adopting this attitude toward conservatives in your life, or an older relative who voted for Donald Trump simply because he was the GOP nominee. I have many people in my family who are like this—they now express regret for supporting Trump. Antagonizing them for having done so would be unproductive.

But there are people and organizations that I'd encourage you to avoid empathizing with. Some of them are obvious—few people would seriously suggest that you should try to see the good in an avowed neo-Nazi, for example. Doing so would only provide them with space and acceptance that they don't deserve, space that they'll use to advocate for violence, racism, and anti-democratic ideals. Chapters 1, 2, and 3 all touch on the fact that once fascists have a foot in the door, they'll use it to wedge themselves in further.

Most political activists, strategists, and organizers agree that fascism needs to be confronted directly when it appears in public. The thing is, confronting fascists will put you in danger. Fascists respond with violence when you try to stop them. This danger is, at a minimum, verbal and psychological. But more worryingly, as I laid out in Chapter 1, fascists won't just resort to physical violence when threatened— they'll eagerly engage in it because they believe it's good for their community and for their members. Fascists relish violence and look for opportunities to be violent. And this is exactly the reason that we need to confront them in public, even though

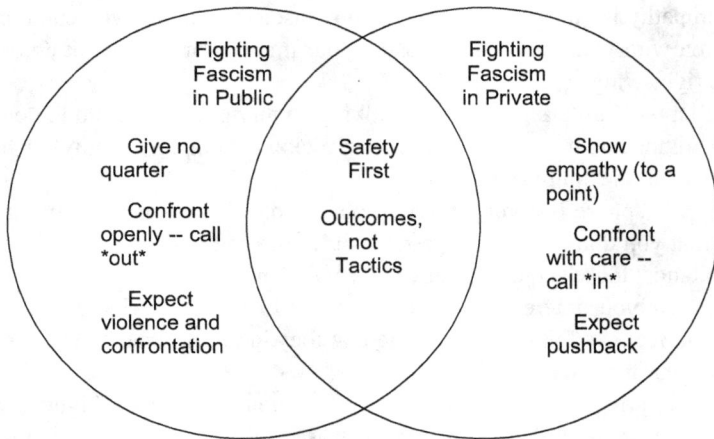

FIGURE 6.1 Here are some of the main differences between how to fight fascism in public and in private. With the exception of this chapter, this book is about how to fight it in private.

Source: Author's creation.

it's dangerous. They can't be allowed to take up space in public because every inch they take is one that they've made unsafe for everyday people.

Fighting Fascism Together

Teaching your son to talk to friends about fascism will mean helping him through a version of what you've learned from reading this book—ways to identify fascist and right-wing ideas, and, most importantly, ways to confront them without assuming that the person saying them is already too far gone. Simply calling out people he knows from school or from the internet for being fascists is only the first step; it's more important to try to help other young men avoid getting recruited by fascists themselves. "Fascist" can't just be another playground insult. Your son needs to understand that it's a serious, adult issue that he and his fellow young men are going to encounter throughout their young lives.

Because fascists are so violent, not just in practice but at the heart of their ideology, confronting them always carries the risk of retaliation. This means that confronting them requires you to have a plan for what to do if they become violent. I'll talk about what that looks like in street-level protests later in this chapter, but here we're talking about the kind of violence your son might experience at school or in other spaces for young people. Calling out friends and classmates could get him insulted or even physically attacked. Work with your son to help him understand those risks, and why they might be worth it in order to stand up to fascism.

You'll need to coach your son through how he can do this work on his own; you can't be there for him every time he encounters fascist or right-wing perspectives or every time one of his peers expresses them. Helping him to deal with these conversations without alienating himself from his friends is a vital part of teaching him to deal with fascism.

The skills and advice built up in this book to help your son stay away from fascism will be very helpful to him in talking with his peers. Teach him how to use empathy as a tool to get at bigotry and when it's time to condemn someone for what they've said or done rather than appealing to their humanity or giving them the benefit of the doubt. These are difficult skills for adults to master, so they'll be tough for your son too. But that doesn't mean that he's not ready; as he becomes a young man, he's old enough to start taking moral responsibilities.

Walk your son through some of the examples in this book. You can even use examples of conversations you've already had with him about right-wing content as guides for how he can talk to peers. Remind him that when he showed an interest in a right-wing influencer or told a racist joke without knowing what it meant, you didn't immediately jump to the conclusion that he was totally lost. Instead, you asked him where he found that content and what he liked about it. You did your best to sound empathetic but principled.

Some of the main tips that I've given already will serve him well. Approaching conversations with his peers with curiosity and without immediate condemnation might help him get engagement from them without shutting them down completely. That will stand a better chance of letting your son work with his peers to help them see what it really is that they're talking about—remembering that most kids who encounter or share right-wing ideas don't really know what they're doing and are just repeating things that they've heard or that caught their attention somehow.

That said, your son will also need to be careful not to let himself get dragged into accepting or respecting these views, a very careful tightrope act. Engaging with what his peers are saying will be more important if he's outnumbered, whereas condemning them would make more sense if he's in a group where most others are on the fence.

Sometimes you and your son will be together when you encounter fascist or extreme right-wing messages. This could happen on the street, as you overhear someone saying something extremist, or it could be seeing fascist or right-wing symbols graffitied on a building or stuck up on someone's car. It could come from a relative at a family event, or it could come from a person on the internet, TV, or radio. In these settings, you'll be there to guide and set the tone for how to respond. If it's physically safe to respond, you should. Call out racism, sexism, homophobia, and fascist messaging when you hear it in public. You can't let those things go unanswered—that's how the fascists feel safer expressing them.

Other times, your son will be without you when he hears or sees these things. This could happen in a locker room or school setting, with friends, or in an online message board, chat, or video. In these situations, you'll need to have prepared your son ahead of time to respond effectively and safely to the fascist messaging. This will mean trusting your son as an ally and friend, and acknowledging that you don't have all the answers or know exactly the right thing to do at all times. Here you'll start to lean on him for help and support, as an equal in the fight against fascism.

Here's a brief, non-exhaustive sample of groups that are fighting fascism around the world:

- The Southern Poverty Law Center and the American Civil Liberties Union monitor fascist and other far right-wing groups in the United States while combating them in the world of law and public relations.
- Hope Not Hate is a UK-based antifascist organization that also works against antisemitism and anti-Islamic hatred.
- There are dozens, if not hundreds, of groups that focus on preventing the spread of disinformation online. One example is Moonshot, already profiled in this book.
- In many countries, prominent leftist parties fight against fascism openly, either through their youth wing or through their main party. If you're interested in this work, look into your local left party.
- Many other antifascist groups aren't formal organizations and are instead intentional, decentralized collectives of neighbors working together to keep themselves and their communities safe. One example in the United States would be Anti-Racist Action. Another is Unicorn Riot, which focuses on online campaigns.

In addition to these groups, I encourage you to join with other community organizations—churches, local parties, unions, social clubs, school organizations, etc.—and build opposition to fascism in them!

Fighting Fascism Safely

If you've set out to fight fascism in public, you need to know exactly what you're getting yourself into and take precautions. There are many books, articles, podcasts, and interviews that will give you some important and useful strategies for this, and I've listed some of them. Here, I have a short summary of their collective advice.

The first is that unless you are dealing with a very, very small number of fascists and you yourself are a large, intimidating man, you shouldn't confront fascists publicly if you are alone. Fascists thrive on violence, particularly public violence against their political enemies. They are known throughout history to confront their opponents both publicly and in ambushes once they have some distance from a crowd. They won't hesitate to use weapons or other means of inflicting serious harm, or even death. This means that if you confront them, you need to be prepared to fight. Note that I say "prepared" and not "eager"—physical violence entering the political world is only good for them, not us. They've shifted our political culture to be more violent already, and we should always count actual violence as a win for them.

If you do plan on confronting fascists in public, you need to be informed. The two biggest things you need to keep in mind are the kind of event you're attending and the kind of fascist that is likely to be there.

Confronting fascists at a rally or event that caters to people who *aren't* fascists is the safer of the two options. Fascists often come to events of groups that they dislike or seek to harm, such as queer rights protests, abortion clinics, drag shows, Black churches, synagogues, and leftist demonstrations, in order to cause psychological and physical harm. However, at these rallies, they are the outsiders and very likely to be outnumbered. This means that while they might be vocal and try to take up space or get media attention, they're unlikely to be earnestly looking for a physical confrontation at the event itself. Instead, their goal will be to make people feel—and be—unsafe in spaces that should be welcoming to them.

In these contexts, some aggression might be warranted. Put yourself between the fascists and the rest of the people at the event and show that the fascists aren't welcome. Tell them with your body and your voice that they shouldn't be there, that they aren't wanted, and that they should leave without coming back. Importantly, though, you need to be sure that you don't make your presence and the verbal violence that you're engaging with the center of the event—making the event about violence, again, is just giving the fascists what they want. Instead, you need to understand yourself as an auxiliary to the real focus of the event and its organizers.

Keeping track of the fascist groups that are likely to attend the event will help you understand what you're potentially getting yourself into. If the rally is being attended by fascist or right-wing policy wonks from a DC think tank, you probably don't need to be prepared for violence. If, instead, it's making the rounds on the right-wing corners of the internet and has garnered a lot of press, then it's possible others will be there instead. Groups to keep an eye out for in the United States include the Proud Boys, the Three Percenters, and people who participate in the "boogaloo" movement. The Proud Boys were covered in Chapter 1—they've been the most successful fascist organization in the United States in the 21st century. These groups are dedicated right-wing street gangs whose goal is to prepare their members for violence. They conduct training in street violence, have drills in street fighting, and carry weapons. These people are a danger to any other person around them.

Things are very, very different if you are trying to confront fascists at an event that they themselves have organized. That means they've planned for violence and are looking forward to it. Events like this would include major fascist and right-wing rallies such as 2017's Unite the Right in Charlottesville or major confrontations at flashpoints like college campuses or large political rallies.

If you're entering a space like this, you need your body to be prepared for it. Whether or not you show up as a peaceful protester, the fascists will see you as a potential target for violence. This experience is not for everyone, and you should only enter it with a plan.

Fascism and the Police

Throughout this book, I've said relatively little about the police and their relationship to fascists—that's because we've so far been focused on fighting fascism at home and in our communities, rather than in public. Now that I'm preparing you to engage with fascism in the street or in public in general, there are some key things we need to address.

The first of these is that no matter what your demographics or your prior relationship with the police, you need to assume that when and if you are out confronting fascists in public, the police are likely to either side with them or treat you all the same. The police are likely to use serious riot control tactics against you, including intentionally corralling people in places or ways that are unlawful in order to justify arrests, shooting you with rubber or other "nonlethal" weapons, and using tear gas or other chemical weapons against you. This is a normal part of how the police deal with any protest and has to be expected.

What might surprise you is that the police are significantly less likely to use any similar force against the fascists you are fighting. This isn't to say that the police don't police fascists—they do, and sometimes very brutally—but there are also numerous cases of direct police collaboration with fascists when it comes to street violence. And I don't just mean that their interests are aligned or that both groups target minorities and other oppressed people. I mean that the police directly engage with fascists to get them to do "dirty work" that would be illegal for the police.

For example, during a wave of fascist activity in Portland, Oregon, after Trump's 2016 victory, the local police chief was in direct contact with the leader of the local Proud Boys chapter. The two of them were texting back and forth, relaying information about where they were and where a new police presence was about to be.[3] For the Proud Boys, this meant that they could avoid being out in the street where the police were likely to be, which allowed them to largely avoid arrest despite the fact that they were engaging in clearly illegal activities. It also meant that they were free to engage in violence with progressives they encountered because they knew that the police wouldn't be around to witness it and be forced to stop them.

Why did the police work with the fascists in this case? There are a number of reasons. The simplest is that the leader of the police and the leader of the Proud Boys were friends and associates, and were known to have hung out over beers together. But that personal explanation begs another question—what was it about these two men's politics, social worlds, and jobs that made it possible for them to be friends? After all, one of them was the leader of a street gang that would later play a large role in an attempted coup against the federal government, and the other was the leader of the local law enforcement.

This is a political question, and it's beyond the scope of this book. Historically, though, the fact is that fascists and local law enforcement often work hand in hand.

I can tell you from personal experience that the police and law enforcement work with fascists, even when they aren't doing so intentionally. I was a graduate student at Berkeley in 2017 when a right-wing pundit named Milo Yiannopoulos came to speak on campus. At the time, he was a leading light on the alt-right, which was high in the news due to its connections with Donald Trump's 2016 victory against Hillary Clinton and the ascendance of right-wing politics throughout the world. Yiannopoulos was, at the time, an out gay man (he has since gone through what he describes as a successful "conversion therapy") who was nevertheless a quasi-fascist demagogue. He advocated for taking rights from women, including the right to choose whether to have an abortion. He was opposed to the rights of trans people and anyone who was gender nonconforming. Most violently, when speaking on college campuses, he and his team would research people who were hiding an aspect of their identity from the public due to a desire for their own safety and would publicize it. During his speeches, he would put their names, faces, and other identifying information on a big screen so that the attendees could take notes and laugh. This included sharing pre-transition images of trans people, with the intention of humiliating them. It also included publicizing the information of students who were in the United States without immigration papers, undocumented students whose ability to remain in the United States partly depended on their not being confronted by law enforcement.

This constituted direct, personal violence against students, staff, and faculty on campus. In addition to the hateful politics that Yiannopoulos held and would express at his rally, this was an extremely good reason to try to stop him from speaking at Berkeley campus.

Along with some other graduate students from my department, I attended this anti-Yiannopoulos rally. The rally to block Yiannopoulos from entering the building where he was to speak escalated into an earnest effort by some of the attendees to make his speaking there impossible. These protesters knew that if certain fire code standards were temporarily broken in the building, it would be impossible for the event to be held. They had some of their allies distract security while they broke into the building and set off the fire alarm, forcing the school to cancel the event.

That day, the police of the city of Berkeley and the university's own robust police force were extremely active. Their goal was to protect Yiannopoulos—though he was never in physical danger and was never at the site—and to allow him to speak. Their goal was not to protect protesters, as they repeatedly threatened to use tear gas or to advance with weapons. Their goal wasn't to protect the students, faculty, and staff whose lives Yiannopoulos planned to endanger with his speech. Their goal was to protect him and his interests, and to protect property.

After Yiannopoulos was turned away, the news stories were about the property destruction committed by the protesters. They had broken some windows, and one person attacked an ATM. These acts of petty property violence stole the headlines from the real people whose lives and safety were at risk because of Yiannopoulos, and denied the bravery of those who stood up against him, risking their criminal records and lives in the process.

This is what you can expect from the police when you're dealing with fascists and fascism—or when you're protesting anything at all, for that matter. This might come as a surprise or shock to those of you who have never been on the other side of the police because of class or racial privileges. My goal with this book isn't to convince you that the police are a vital part of the repression conducted by the US government. I mention these stories to show you, from experience, that this is what you should expect if you try to combat fascism. Often—all too often—the police will not be on your side.

Other Ways to Fight Fascism

You may be reading this chapter and thinking that this fighting fascism in the streets thing isn't for you—after all, it's a dangerous enterprise that involves confronting very dangerous people. I can't and don't blame people for deciding that this kind of fight against fascism isn't for them. That's one of the main reasons I wrote this book, in the hopes of showing people that there are many ways to stop fascism from growing in our homes and communities.

But if street confrontation doesn't sound like your method for fighting fascism, don't worry! There are so many more things you can do to help stop the rise of fascism in your public life. Many of them also involve your son, other children, and family.

The first and most necessary step is that you need to call out fascism when you see it in your peer group. When a colleague, a fellow parent, or a relative says or does something that is white supremacist, misogynist, or nationalistic, it's your job to say something about it. Keeping your safety in mind, determine whether or not you're in a situation where it's safe to directly confront this messaging. For example, if you're in a bar full of strangers who seem to agree with the person talking, it's not the best time to talk about the dangers of fascism. Just indicate that you don't agree and leave.

But if you're in a safer environment—at work or in a school board meeting, for example—you can be more direct. When you're not at a street protest, remember that yelling or being aggressive is likely unnecessary and will backfire against you when you're dealing with right-wing messaging. You want to appear to be the more reasonable people in the room.

The best way to do this is by knowing more about right-wing politics than the right-wingers themselves do. If you know the ins and outs of the conspiracy theory they're sprouting or the racist trope they're engaging in, you can sometimes literally talk circles around them. Get to their conspiracy point before they do, and refute it before they can make it. Deny them the ability to go through their normal rote conversation on the topic. And above all, be sure that everybody in the room knows you disagree and aren't a part of what they're saying. When it comes to fascism and the right-wing, it's vital that people see that there are those who disagree and aren't following along. Otherwise, the crowd you're with might get the impression that the terrible things that being said are more commonly accepted than they should be, which is a big part of how they become normalized.

In these environments, and dealing with equals rather than your children, you can adopt a position that's between the empathy I've suggested for a son who's gotten into fascism and the direct confrontation that I'll suggest for when you're dealing with fascists who are out in public. Remember, your goal isn't to convince the person you're talking to that they're wrong—you'll likely never be able to do that, given how entrenched people are in their positions. That doesn't mean that you should avoid talking to them about their ideas altogether, though. It's important that you show you disagree with them, and that you don't accept what they're saying.

The conversation might go something like this:

COWORKER: I was driving my kid to their soccer practice this weekend, and the app told me to go through, you know, that neighborhood—by the time I realized where it was taking us we were already late! But I had to turn around, they missed the first ten minutes of the game.
YOU: Sorry, I don't understand—what neighborhood do you mean?
COWORKER: You know, x neighborhood.
YOU: Why would you need to avoid that part of town?
COWORKER: Come on.
YOU: No sorry, I don't get it. Why would you not want to go there?

This kind of conversation forces people to express their biases and prejudices out loud, which they tend to find uncomfortable to the point that they might stop saying them in front of you or in front of others in the environment you were in. It's even possible that this might get the person you're talking to to question their biases—they may never have said them out loud before!

What if you're dealing with someone who is more clearly in the right-wing world? That conversation might go something more like this:

RIGHT-WINGER: I just can't wait till the left is out of power. Then maybe we can get something done in this country
YOU: I don't want the [insert your country's progressive party] out of power—they protect rights that are important to me and my family.
RIGHT-WINGER: Oh, so you're one of those?
YOU: Ha, I'm not sure what you mean. Those what?

RIGHT-WINGER:	Those liberals.
YOU:	Well, if by that you mean that I don't want vulnerable people to not have the protection and safety they deserve, then yeah, I guess I am. What do you think?
RIGHT-WINGER:	I think we should send them all away! (this is the most mild way such a person might express a similar bias—they might literally come out and say that they want to kill certain people at this point)
YOU:	Yeah, I don't agree with you at all on this, and we're not going to get anywhere. You should think about what it was that led you to this point in your life, that you're willing to talk about hurting others.

The point of this conversation isn't to change the mind of the person you're talk-ing to. You need to assume that their mind has been made up to the point that they won't listen to you or anyone else's arguments, at least in public.

When it comes to arguing with people, think about formal debates like court-rooms or the kinds of debate societies they have at Oxford. In these settings, there are two sides, and both of them are obligated to promote their case above the other by any means necessary. Their goal isn't to convince each other but to convince the audience—the jury or the other members of the debate club. Their opponent will never admit defeat on their own, and no evidence they can give or perspective they can share will get the opposition to acknowledge that they've lost.

Debating in regular life is actually a lot like this too. Your opponent will almost never turn to you and say that you've made them change their mind. They'll prob-ably dig in their heels and deny the evidence you give or turn to debate tactics that insult you personally. If they're right-wing, they might start to threaten you or peo-ple you care about. Your job is to greet this behavior with calm resolve.

If this person is a friend or someone you're close to and trust, they might hear you out and realize that what they're saying is harmful or problematic. They might take your words to heart. Alternatively, and honestly more likely, they might just decide that talking to you about these subjects isn't worth it and will stop bringing them up around you. That may not be an ideal outcome, but it's an acceptable one when it comes to protecting your son from fascist ideology.

Remember that when you're in conversations with your peers about politics, your goal isn't to convince them they're wrong on the spot—that's not how debates work. If you ever did high school debate, or Model UN, or anything similar—or if you've ever seen a movie about a trial—you know that the two sides in a debate rarely concede during the conversation itself. Both sides are there to represent themselves as best as possible in the moment, so that the other people there can decide how well they've done. This is the reason that being the calmer, kinder per-son in a debate is so important! Acting this way might infuriate the person you're talking to, but it'll make you look like the more reasonable person to anybody around you. Remember, *they're* the people you're trying to get on your side, *not* the person you're debating.

The need to stand up against fascism in public extends to social media and the online world, too. When you see something that sounds right-wing, call it out. Sheltering yourself from it or ignoring it will not make it go away.

Fascism and Mainstream Politics

If you are in the United States, or in another Western country, then you are likely living through the most troubling growth of right-wing sentiment that your country has seen since WWII. Openly extreme right-wing candidates are winning elections across the world and are appealing to more and more voters. They're entering political coalitions with mainstream conservatives and changing what people think of as normal or acceptable politics.

One of the main ways that they do this comes in the form of working with conservatives. Remembering Chapter 1, we know that fascists have never taken power in a country without the help of the rest of the right-wing—namely, the more moderate and centrist parts of the right-wing. These groups are not themselves fascists and often disagree with some of the more extreme parts of fascist ideology. However, they'll work with fascists if they think it'll be beneficial to them. First, they'll use fascists to do their dirty work. In the United States, this looks like conservative GOP groups using the Proud Boys and other fascist organizations as "security" for their events, or like Donald Trump relying on them to stage his attempted coup on January 6. Fascist and extreme right-wing groups also do some legislative dirty work by proposing bills and measures that the conservatives wouldn't want to be directly tied to themselves but which they might pass to "appease" their allies, throwing up their hands and saying they had no other choice.

This means that fascists don't come alone. They have allies and political networks they work through; they have the whole conservative base that they can try to move in their direction. And they have natural political allies when it comes to mainstream conservatives.

I wish I could say that those of us who are fighting fascism also have such natural allies, but sadly I can't. Most centrist and leftist politicians in the United States, Europe, and other Western countries try to ignore or avoid the problem of fascism rather than confronting it head-on. There are some notable exceptions, of course— Biden and the Democratic establishment were acceptably serious about prosecuting the participants in the January 6, 2021, attempted coup in the United States. They also made gestures toward holding some elected officials accountable for their involvement in it. But they still fell far short of the ideal. They wouldn't call it an attempted coup, and they tip-toed around prosecuting Trump for his involvement. Conversely, in Brazil, former President Jair Bolsonaro was rendered ineligible to run for political office for eight years due to his much less direct involvement in a similar attempted coup on January 8, 2023.

The Democrats' reluctance to call out fascism and the extreme right-wing for what they are stems from their political position. They don't want to move too far left because their business interests wouldn't support it. That means they need to move to the right to pick up some centrists and moderate conservatives. We can clearly see this with the rightward policy drift of the Democratic Party starting in the 1980s and most pronouncedly in the 1990s with the Clinton presidency. The "common sense" here is that voters need to be followed rather than pushed—that voters and the public can't be convinced of things and that the best we can do politically is to follow what the opinion polls say.

I'm here to tell you that the right-wing *doesn't do that*, and they get what they want. Instead of just following the public, they try to lead it. They engage in political work and propaganda whose goal is to change minds and convince people that they are right. If you want to stop fascism, you need to do the same, and you need to demand that your political parties do it too. Moving right to win the next election only means that the country will be further away from what you want next time.

There have been times in history when moderates and the left have come together to fight fascism or to block it from taking power. In the 1930s, this kind of politics was called a "popular front," meaning that two groups who normally disagree with each other very much, like leftists and centrists, united against the fascists and the right-wing. This was the basis of the alliance among the United States, the United Kingdom, and the Soviet Union during WWII—three countries with different economic and political systems uniting to stop fascism in Europe and the rest of the world. It's also been the basis of several domestic political coalitions, especially those that unite the center and the far left in the interest of shutting out the extreme right-wing.

Since the post-war era, there haven't been that many "popular fronts" that really deserve the name—and that's a shame! This is exactly the sort of thing that we need in order to stop fascism today. And that's especially true in places where the political left isn't powerful enough to stop fascism on its own. In these cases, the left will really need the help of the center and possibly even the mainstream right-wing to keep the fascists and the rest of the far right out of power. This looks different at different times, but the general rule is that the parts of the coalition agree that fascism is so dangerous and such a threat to everyone's safety that it needs to be confronted by everyone at once, working together.

Sadly, as you probably already knew even before you started reading this book, most people fail to understand the dangers of fascism even when it is staring them in the face. They'll deny that it's a danger or that it is fascism or that fascism needs to be excluded from the world of politics.

When it comes to fighting fascism at the ballot box, you have a tough choice to make. Politicians and parties that openly discuss fascism and the need to stop the extreme right-wing are few and far between, especially in the world's biggest democracies. Far more common are large centrist parties of either the left or the right that occasionally lean to one side or the other, depending on which way the wind is blowing. That means that, sadly, you'll have to do a similar kind of evaluation yourself when elections arrive. If your primary goal, or even one of your bigger goals as a voter, is to stop fascism, you'll need to choose whether you vote for a party that directly confronts fascism or just for one that might stymie it simply by winning against it. In the United States, this might look like the choice between voting for a candidate like Bernie Sanders, who openly and directly talks about the need to fight fascism and the far right, and a candidate like Hillary Clinton, Joe Biden, or Kamala Harris, who oppose fascism because they're establishment candidates who don't want the radical changes that fascists are proposing. Outside the United States or the United Kingdom, you might have more leftist parties to vote for, such as Die Linke in Germany or the Partido Socialismo e Liberdade in Brazil. Still, the choice is roughly the same—do you vote for the party you actually want, the one that is openly confronting fascism, or a more centrist party that has a greater chance of winning?

I won't claim to answer this question for you. It'll depend on your own politics, the situation in your country, and the current political landscape during that election cycle. I will say, though, that when there are no political parties or politicians who openly and directly oppose fascism, it's much harder for a society to really oppose it.

Healthy, Diverse Communities Stop Fascism

One of the most important ways you can help your son avoid engaging with right-wing perspectives is by making sure that he's part of healthier, more diverse communities that have no space for these beliefs.

Sadly, many parents in the United States and other developed countries might find this difficult. Most of the community spaces available to people in the United States are themselves segregated by race or gender—for example, churches and schools are often highly racially segregated, while sports teams are segregated by gender. This means that they can be a good place for unexamined biases to develop and spread, and these are exactly the kinds of things that can lead to increasingly right-wing beliefs. The isolation of suburban life, the most common environment for young people in the United States and in much of the rest of the developed world, means that often their opportunities for community are limited to these likely segregated in-person ones and online communities. As discussed in the previous chapter, these communities are especially prone to right-wing thinking because of their lack of diversity, and in the case of online communities, the distance and anonymity they give to their members.

Ensuring that your son is part of a diverse community means that you'll need to be part of one too—it's not enough to tell your son about the benefits of diversity for his development. Making diversity a central pillar of your family values is one of the best ways that you can help show your son the importance of not isolating yourself only among people who are just like you or among people you agree with completely. This won't be an easy task, especially in the United States, where public and private spaces are typically very segregated by race and class.

Actually practicing diversity in your everyday life will mean some significant changes to your routines and lifestyles. It might mean choosing not to live in an isolated suburb and instead living in a metropolitan area where your son will meet and interact with people of different races and ethnicities. It might mean changing which church or other religious institution you attend. It might mean sending your son to public school rather than a private one, especially if the private/public school divide in your area is entirely class-driven.

Sports and extracurriculars are another, even thornier topic when it comes to diversity, specifically regarding sex and gender. If your son's primary school community is a football team, then it's simply more likely that the perspectives he hears from his peers will be those of other cisgender men. This holds true for most other sex- and gender-segregated activities, like the Boy Scouts or other sports teams. Not only is the lack of diversity in these activities an issue, but it's well known that they are a breeding ground for the baseline sexism and bigotry that can make people more accepting of the extreme right-wing.

Pursuing diversity in your community and your son's community is the sort of thing you can do to prevent right-wing sentiments from developing in him. If you try to use this tactic *after* your son has already developed right-wing thinking, it'll be much harder for you to convince him that it's worthwhile. This is because the right-wing argues that diversity is a false virtue. At their most moderate, they'll say that diversity is a value pushed on white people rather than people of color. Or they might argue that the countries that are being encouraged to celebrate diversity are historically white, whereas other societies aren't similarly encouraged to do so. At their most radical, they'll argue that diversity is a tool used by some "global elite" to control societies and to transform them into different, subservient ones dominated by foreign ideologies.

If your son is already far enough along in right-wing politics, then putting him in more diverse circumstances may have the opposite effect of what you intend. It might convince him that you've been captured by some sort of antagonistic agent that opposes his identity or his heritage, or at least that you've fallen prey to their ideology. Appeals to the value of diversity would fall on deaf ears if the kid in question is already a fascist, or if he's already on the side of people who think that diversity isn't just unnecessary but actively harmful.

Having a diverse community might reduce the likelihood that you encounter fascism in your daily life, but it won't prevent it. You can still have fascists in your life at work, in a religious community, or in your extended family. If you have a fascist or right-wing relative in your family, first of all, I want to express my sympathy, and my experiences with the same. Dealing with the fascism of an adult in your family is difficult in entirely different ways than it is with a child.

Fighting fascism together means recognizing that any problems with the right-wing you may be experiencing in your family are part of a bigger picture—we're all dealing with this right now, in our families, communities, and countries. When I wrote this book, it was with the hope that if you were motivated to keep your son out of the right-wing, it was because you don't want the extreme right-wing to have power in our society, and not just because you don't want that for your son. You know that the far right is a particularly dangerous thing, and that its power or dominance in our culture could lead to catastrophic changes.

Throughout this chapter, and the rest of this book, I've been linking fascism with the ideologies it is so often combined with—racism, sexism, anti-queer ideologies, and other forms of discrimination. The strategies I've talked about in this chapter don't just apply to fully fledged fascist mobilization. They will help to combat all those connected ideologies too. Like I said in Chapter 1, if it quacks like a duck, call it a duck.

I spoke with Aaron Winter, a sociologist who studies race and the far right and is currently a Senior Lecturer (Professor) of Criminology at the University of East London. The grandchild of Holocaust survivors who fled first to Bolivia and then to Canada, Winter said that he was educated as an antifascist in his youth. "Fascism and racism were part of the ongoing discussion at home, and part of my identity. I grew up during the skinhead revival in Toronto—my friends were racially and class mixed, and we'd get chased or attacked by the skinheads pretty often."

Winter says that these experiences led him to what would end up being his academic focus—exposing the links between the extreme right and the everyday racism, sexism, and classism that affect people. "I remember one time hanging out with my diverse crowd of friends, some Black, most of us working class, when a group of skinheads showed up. They were smaller in number, but they chased us through the street and onto the Toronto subway. We ran into some police and asked them for help, but then they looked at us. For a number of reasons—how we were dressed, the fact that we were a mixed group, and our age—they treated us like we were the ones causing the trouble."

Experiences like that taught Winter about the connection between the far right and the everyday ways that the government treats people of color, women, and working-class people. "My friends at the time who were Black, who were young women, or gay, what they were seeing from the police and from the skinheads wasn't that different." Even as a teen, though, Winter didn't just equate the two. "We knew who had power in society."

From these experiences as a youth, Winter developed an interest in explaining how the mainstream world uses fascists to do their dirty work. In *Reactionary Democracy*, he and his co-author Aurelien Mondon argue that the far right serves the mainstream in two ways. One, which I've talked about already in this book, is that when the far right gets powerful enough, they can do the dirty work that the government doesn't want to be directly associated with. They can attack leftists or feminists, while mainstream conservatives can claim that they had nothing to do with it. This was what fascism did for the conservatives in Germany, Italy, and Spain prior to WWII.

But Winter has another, more damning critique of the relationship between the far right and the mainstream. He argues that the extreme right-wing is used as a scapegoat and distraction.

By this, he doesn't mean to downplay the fact that fascists and the far right are a danger. His family history, his own experiences, and his research make that clear. Instead, he means that focusing too much on the extreme right can keep us from seeing the everyday racism, sexism, and classism that the people around us express. And worse, it can distract us from seeing or fighting the much more common ways that our governments and employers prey on exactly the same people that fascists do. "It's important to illustrate to people that the far right is a threat, but there are lots of other ways that democracy is threatened," he says.

By focusing too much on the threat of fascists, though, we can lose sight of how the rest of the systems in our lives do the same harm that the far right and fascists do. By focusing too much on "kids with swastika tattoos," we might start to see the everyday violence that police engage in against people of color as being somehow less important or less dangerous to our society. And the attention we pay to the individual experiences of people who've engaged in right-wing violence can keep us from seeing the systemic forces at work. "I'm less worried about individuals than I am about the wider ecosystem."

Instead of treating the far right like an exception, he says, we have to treat it as another symptom of a bigger problem—the fact that our society as a whole is sexist, racist, and classist, along with hundreds of other ways that it discriminates against people and keeps them from enjoying the rights and privileges they deserve. We have to be careful not to lean too far into accepting the right-wing's own claims that its problems and feelings are special.

Like I've said before, this tension made me very uncomfortable when writing this book. I don't want you to come away from reading this too focused on the problems of young, mostly straight, mostly cis, mostly white men—these are the people who benefit the most from how our society is organized! While they are victims of right-wing radicalization, they aren't the main victims of the right-wing. Those are people of color, women, queer people, trans people, the working class, and the poor. In our private lives, we love and care about the people who are closest to us, but when we turn our eyes outward and look to the rest of society, we shouldn't be fooled into thinking that the biggest problems for the people closest to us are the biggest problems for everyone else too.

I wrote this book in the hopes that it would help you keep your son from continuing this pattern of oppression. As a parent, educator, or other important figure in a young man's life, you're already focusing on the wellbeing and life of a young man. You're already parenting, teaching, or mentoring him, so be sure you're doing it in a way that keeps him out of fascism and helps him to become an antifascist ally.

I hope that you finish this last chapter with a bigger picture in mind about why you should talk to your son about fascism. It's not just for him or for you and your family. It's for all of us. And if you care enough to keep your son out of fascism because of how it affects the people who are already the most disadvantaged in our society, then I hope you also vote, donate, and work on those wider problems too. Together, we can keep ourselves safe and help to build a more tolerant, joyful, and freer world.

Notes

1 Valeri, Robin Maria, Sweazy, Nicole E., and Borgeson, Kevin, "An Analysis of Skin-head Websites and Social Networks, a Decade Later," *Michigan Sociological Review* 31 (2017): 76–105. www.jstor.org/stable/26284785.
2 Bresciani, Marco, *Learning from the Enemy: An Intellectual History of Antifascism in Interwar Europe*. 1st ed. New York: Verso Books, 2024; Fronczak, Joseph, *Everything Is Possible*. Unabridged ed. Tantor Media, Inc., 2023; García, Hugo, Yusta, Mercedes, Tabet, Xavier, and Clímaco, Christina, eds., *Rethinking Antifascism: History, Memory and Political Uses, 1922 to the Present*. New York: Berghahn Books, 2016; Plum, Catherine J., *Antifascism After Hitler: East German Youth and Socialist Memory, 1949–1989*. New York: Routledge, 2015; Chamedes, Giuliana, "How to Do Things with Words: Antifascism as a Differentially Mobilizing Ideology, from the Popular Front to the Black Power Movement," *Journal of the History of Ideas* 84, no. 1 (2023): 127–55; Gottfried, Paul. *Antifascism: The Course of a Crusade*. 1st ed. Ithaca: Cornell University Press, 2021; Burley, Shane. *Why We Fight: Essays on Fascism, Resistance, and Surviving the Apocalypse*. Foreword by Natasha Lennard. Chico, CA: AK Press, 2021; Burley, Shane, ed., *No Pasarán: Antifascist Dispatches from a World in Crisis*. Foreword by Tal Lavin. Afterword by David Renton. Chico, CA: AK Press, 2022; Hope, Jeanelle K., and Mullen, Bill V., *The Black Antifascist Tradition: Fighting Back from Anti-Lynching to Abolition*. Chicago, IL: Haymarket Books, 2023.
3 Ortiz, Eric, "'Disturbing' Texts Between Oregon Police and Far-Right Group Prompt Investigation," *NBC News*, February 15, 2019. The police chief was later acquitted in this investigation.

INDEX

Note: Page numbers in *italic* indicate a figure on the corresponding page.

For Product Safety Concerns and Information please contact our EU
representative GPSR@taylorandfrancis.com
Taylor & Francis Verlag GmbH, Kaufingerstraße 24, 80331 München, Germany

www.ingramcontent.com/pod-product-compliance
Lightning Source LLC
Chambersburg PA
CBHW071747270326
41928CB00013B/2824

9 781032 472539